SHOW ME . . .
NATURE'S WRATH

BY
DON CORRIGAN

REEDY PRESS
St. Louis, Missouri

Reedy Press
PO Box 5131
St. Louis, MO 63139, USA

Library of Congress Control Number: 2009938062

ISBN: 978-1-933370-81-1

Please visit our website at www.reedypress.com.

Cover design by Kevin Belford

Printed in the United States of America
09 10 11 12 13   5 4 3 2 1

Contents

ACKNOWLEDGMENTS

As this book project gets prepped for some ink, I watch from my office window as the prevailing westerlies blow in weather from the Great Plains and Mountain States. Trees and greenery are bending reluctantly to the east, as brisk winds blow in more summer thunder showers. Summer 2009 has been another wet one, as can be readily observed on the local rivers and lakes that I kayak and sail. Dam spillways are opened wide. Shores are more distant when traversing the water. Trees and vegetation along the shorelines are green and lush, but sometimes they are half-submerged in fresh water—recently fallen from thunderous skies. Is this the way it is going to be in the Midwest now that global warming seems to be having its way with our climate? Or is this just the quirkiness of a certain moment in the infinite unfolding of continual weather change?

Those questions are for more expert minds, but I would like to offer here my first and foremost acknowledgment—to nature. During the course of writing this book, nature has kept me vitally interested in its most important activity—the weather. Nature's work and play in the skies has kept me focused throughout this writing adventure. Flooding in the spring of 2008 in St. Louis urged me to the bluffs of Sunset Hills to watch the Meramec River cover large parts of Fenton. A spectacular view of the rising water was occasionally obstructed by snow showers. Later in the year, lightning in Kansas City had me talking to lightning rod experts and emergency personnel. In early 2009, AmeriCorps volunteers shared stories of what they encountered while helping Bootheel residents get through one of the state's most severe ice storms. Late spring of 2009 brought tornadoes to southwest Missouri and to Kirksville. A hailstorm in the Joplin area, at about the same time, prompted several residents to send me odd photos of ice balls covering the landscape. The straight-line windstorm of May 8, 2009, resulted in some incredible damage to timber stock in the state, and I was able to witness the damage firsthand on forest trails in southern Missouri. Yes, nature's weather antics have kept me focused on this book project from start to finish, and that surely needs to be acknowledged.

Professionals who have dedicated their lives to minding the weather—television meteorologists—have been primary sources in compiling material for this book. Television weather forecasters from around the state responded to a survey conducted in the summer of 2008. The survey asked for their views on Missouri's weather events. Soon, many of these meteorologists were e-mailing descriptions of the most noteworthy tornadoes, floods, hailstorms, lightning strikes, blizzards, and ice storms in their television market areas. Newspaper clips and archival material followed. A special thanks must go out to: Kristen Cornett, Kent Ehrhardt, John Fuller, Dave Murray, and Cindy Preszler of St. Louis; Bryan Busby, Gary Lezak, Jeff Penner, and Lisa Teachman of Kansas City; Eric Aldrich, Josh deBerge, and Zach Paul of the Columbia–Jefferson City area; Gary Bandy and Dave Snider of the Joplin-Springfield area; Brian Alworth and Bob Reeves of Cape Girardeau.

Also instrumental in helping get this book put together were Pat Guinan, a climatologist with the University of Missouri Extension Service, and James Kramper of the NOAA National Weather Service Office for the St. Louis region. Kramper was extremely helpful in providing direction to weather photo archives and data sources in the public domain on the Internet. Guinan also provided pointers on weather data available for the state of Missouri.

Reedy Press provided an abundance of encouragement and patience in working out the publication details of this book. Josh Stevens and Matt Heidenry deserve a special thanks, as does the Reedy researcher Don Korte and 2009 summer intern Kathy Frank, a student at DePaul University, who did yeoman's work in sleuthing many of the images to accompany the weather sketches.

My friends, colleagues, and students at Webster University, where I have taught for three decades, provided valuable assistance. The Environmental Studies Committee includes dedicated faculty who keep a close eye on weather and flooding issues, such as David A. Wilson with Environment & Community Planning at the East-West Gateway Council of Governments. Other committee faculty include: Lori Diefenbacher, Jeff DePew, Don Conway-Long, Kate Parsons, Dani McCartney, Paul Moriarty, Gerry Tierney, Steve Hinson, Karla Armbruster, Jih-un Kim, Allan MacNeill, Stephanie Schroeder, and Tim Green.

Webster University journalism student Colleen Reany provided a firsthand account of getting washed out of her home in a flash flood by the remnants of Hurricane Ike in 2008. Kerry McMahon, now at the University of Maryland, helped with research as well as format and layout ideas for the book. Other Webster students who offered support included Chris Birk, Kelly Kendall, Jonathon Webb, Jenn Proffitt, Kholood Eid, Matt Blickenstaff, Jon Baird, Kelly Atherton, Nikole Brown, Anna Forder, Kevin Huelsmann, Brittany Whitlow, Amber Russell, Jack Czarnecki, Liz Miller, Alex Bates, Andrea Sisney, Karen Myers, and many more.

My friends and colleagues at the *Webster-Kirkwood Times/South County Times* are always patient and supportive of my extracurricular activities. Past weather stories by Dwight Bitikofer, Kevin Murphy, Marty Harris, and Fran Mannino provided useful information, whether from the St. Louis snowstorm of 1982 or floods of 2008 on Deer Creek. *Times* intern Erin Smith, from Drake University, helped with research. Photo editor Diana Linsley provided tips on *Times* archival photography.

Finally, I have to express a debt of gratitude to the many service clubs, colleges, high schools, churches, libraries, state parks, nature groups, and bookstores that hosted me when my first Reedy book came out in 2007, *Show Me . . . Natural Wonders*. Many of these same organizations have already invited me back for an encore lecture and discussion with this new project. I'm looking forward to it! Who knows? We may not only talk about the weather—we may do something about it.

Introduction

"**I**'ve lived in a good climate, and it bores the hell out of me," observed the great wordsmith of the hot and gritty Dust Bowl, John Steinbeck. "I like weather, rather than climate," Steinbeck added. No one who has experienced the Missouri climate for any stretch of time could credibly accuse its mercurial weather of the offense of being boring. Every year, the weather in the Show Me State is different; every single season brings its own kind of wild weather excitement. Steinbeck would be pleased that this book focuses on weather that scares the hell out of people rather than weather that bores the hell out of people. These pages provide sketches of nature's wrath spanning decades, and in some cases, reaching back through the centuries. This work is not meant to be an authoritative chronicle but rather a sampler of some of the awesome weather events that have had a memorable impact on Missouri.

Naturally, this compendium of nature's rage must begin with tornadoes. Missouri skies have spawned some of the most fearsome and wondrous weather cyclones known to man, including the horrible 1925 Tri-State Tornado that killed more than 680 people.

Tornadoes are usually profiled as a single, twisting rope that spins across the countryside. In Missouri history, tornadoes have taken on the form of giant bowls, whips, mushrooms, and hourglasses. In intense rainstorms, they have been virtually impossible to see. The infamous Hopkins outbreak of 1881 involved multiple twisters dropping out of the skies. Perhaps the scariest and ugliest tornado catastrophe was in St. Louis in 1896, as documented in the book *The Great Cyclone*. Journalists of the time wrote about its entry into the metropolis as if it were a living monster, complete with body and tail.

Show Me . . . Nature's Wrath also examines the various accoutrements that accompany tornadic storms, such as lightning and hail. A unique voice of Missouri can be found in the anecdotes of the state's lightning rod installers, who provide accounts of great blue bolts hitting trees, church spires, and the state capitol. That same voice is apparent in the hail tales of Missouri—stories about plagues of ice balls pelting pedestrians, shattering windows, and rattling nerves.

Captain Noah of the unsinkable Ark may have performed admirably in the great rain storm of his time, but he has no monopoly on confronting flood problems. Residents of the Missouri region have been dealing with untamed waters since before statehood. In recent decades, flooding in the state has intensified and has been more widespread. This book provides several different perspectives on those especially wet years of 1993 and 2008.

Missouri does not have the protracted blizzards of the upper Midwest or the Rocky Mountain states. A few meteorologists maintain that winter weather events in Missouri should be more properly labeled as snowstorms. Okay. Let us try this on for size: Over the past one hundred years, Missouri has had its share of momentous snowstorms with blizzard-like conditions. State skies have had a peculiar bend toward producing "thundersnows," including several covered in this book: Cape Girardeau in 1979, St. Louis in 1982, and Columbia in 2006.

If it's not about snow, it's all about ice, when it comes to winter storms in Missouri. Ice storms in 2006, 2008, and 2009 knocked out power in wide swaths of the state. Friends and relatives without electricity or heat were forced to bunk up with more fortunate friends and relatives until ice storm damage was repaired. That's what makes these stressful storms especially memorable: unexpected guests and unanticipated intimacy that strained even the most solid relationships with next of kin.

Show Me . . . Nature's Wrath concludes with coverage of some of the prime sizzling heat waves and vicious cold snaps in the state's history. Missouri takes up a prominent portion of middle earth with regard to its location on the vast North American continent. The land reacts to the coming and going of the sun by readily absorbing heat in the summer and shedding all that warmth with winter. In any given year, Missouri residents have to be prepared for both extreme heat and extreme cold. They also must be prepared for soaring heat indexes when the humidity is high, and deadly wind chills with the arrival of Alberta Clippers from Canada's great white north. As accounts in this book reveal, the Grim Reaper's wrath reaches a high point with summer heat waves. The "Dirty Thirties" and the "Fire-box Fifties" were decades of the twentieth century when heat in Missouri was particularly deadly.

A book's introduction is a grand location for seasoned writers to anticipate the hot breath of critics and the chilly reception of assorted reviewers. With that in mind, a few provisos are in order:

- Sketches of nature's wrath in this book are meant to be a sampling of events in Missouri, not the definitive catalog of the worst of wind, rain, and fury. The book is meant as a catalyst for conversation, discussion, and recollection. Such parlance will undoubtedly bring to light omissions of great weather disasters that deserve mention in any authoritative accounting of Missouri meteorological mayhem.

- A case can be made that this work gives an unfair portrait of the particulars of the Show Me State climate. Objection sustained. This book doesn't pretend to give a fair and balanced accounting of how often the weather is fair in the state. It should be noted emphatically that Missourians are not constantly running for cover from tornadoes nor desperately treading water in flash floods.

• New Age sensibilities may bristle at the suggestion that nature can exhibit rage or that weather can be vengeful. Weather just is—and should not be demonized as a sort of wrathful, satanic force. That point is surely worth pondering, although I would challenge any weather shaman to remain stoic in the face of an F5 tornado.

In the course of researching this book, I was amused to find several press accounts about Tom Overby, a visionary who wants a 650-foot-tall tornado monument erected in Kansas City. Twenty feet taller than the Gateway Arch, the spiral structure would include a pinnacle restaurant and would act as a tourism magnet rather than merely as a macabre reminder of the destructive forces of nature.

If Kansas City gets a tornado for tourism, then I would surely favor a massive hailstone monument in Columbia to commemorate the storm of 1919. Jefferson City surely deserves a lightning monument to recall the horrid bolt that took out the statehouse in 1911. Springfield and Sikeston merit giant, glazed oak tree memorials to recall the ice storms they endured in the first decade of a new century.

As a weather fanatic, I am willing to jump on all these meteorological monument bandwagons to celebrate nature's excess, but for now I must simply offer this humble tome of stories recalling nature's wrath in Missouri.

SHOW ME . . .
NATURE'S WRATH

I. Tornadoes

Missouri has an amazing and terrifying tornado history. Rural counties, sprawling suburbs, and densely populated cities have all been hit by nature's most violent vortex creations at some point in time. And, as cable television's Weather Channel is so fond of reminding us, it could happen again—tomorrow, in fact.

It's disturbing to take in the details of these destructive storms. It's chilling to contemplate the impact tornadoes have had on the lives of Missourians who have lived through their twisting, primordial terror.

- Imagine the panic of searching madly for the sturdiest structure in the town of Marshfield in 1880. You have children in tow and the locomotive roar of a twister right behind you. Its gyrating tail is gaining on you.

- Imagine the horror of sitting on your farm house front porch in 1881—isolated in northwest Missouri—and witnessing multiple twisters dropping out of dark skies on your southwest horizon.

- Imagine the fear you would feel if you were on the Mississippi River in an unsteady craft in 1896 when a deadly twister turns east to cross the water from the St. Louis shoreline to Illinois, taking out pieces of the Eads Bridge in the process.

- Imagine the empty feeling in the pit of your stomach after the tornado destruction of Pierce City in 2003. You run up a street in shambles, looking for any survivors. Then you spy the building that was supposed to be the town's storm shelter, collapsed in a heap of bricks and splintered wood.

Tornadoes inevitably capture the imagination of kids growing up in the Midwest. A bit of this phenomenon can be attributed to the spring ritual of watching the movie classic *The Wizard of Oz*. A curious youngster soon learns that Dorothy's Kansas and Tornado Alley are not that far away.

The screaming tornado that took Dorothy Gale to Oz took this writer to my own fantasy land at an early age. Even before I entered kindergarten, I took strange enjoyment in "playing tornado" in the basement of the neighbor girl across the street.

How do you play tornado?

Well, you spin around with your arms out until you're quite dizzy and wobbly. You knock over everything that's standing: building blocks, doll houses, baby carriages, toy stoves, and toy refrigerators. You keep spinning until everything is a grand mess, and you drop to the floor with nausea.

Sometimes in my unusually quiet St. Louis suburb, it wasn't just a matter of "playing tornado." I can still recall one evening when there was a roar of wind outside, large hail was crashing against window panes, and the TV picture was extinguished to a little white dot as all the lights went dark. My family headed to the basement by flashlight. We listened to the commotion outside and hoped for the best.

I can remember a drive through St. Louis a few days later to eyeball the aftermath of the storm that came to be known as the 1959 Gaslight Square Tornado. We were "gawking"—with noses pressed to car windows to get a full view of the February storm's mighty destruction.

Gawking is sometimes described as loutish behavior. There are times when it may be inconsiderate, but it's also a natural reaction. There is an innate curiosity in man to examine the impact of nature's wrath. The scenes of devastation inspire wonder, and they can spur artistic creation and scientific discovery.

A killer tornado in 1879 is said to have inspired newspaperman L. Frank Baum to write the magical story *The Wizard of Oz*. More than a century later, tornado "storm chasers" became the theme for the top-grossing 1996 movie *Twister*. That Hollywood film then became the basis for the popular attraction "Twister . . . Ride It Out," at the Universal Studios Orlando Resort in Florida.

Thanks to the wizardry behind the ride in Orlando, my kids' acquaintance with tornadoes is not confined to a car drive in a neighborhood where homes have lost roofs and tree limbs are down. They wear "Twister . . . Ride It Out" T-shirts and they know much more about the power of tornadic storms than I did as a youngster.

Tornadoes and their devastation also have inspired scientists and meteorologists in a quest to improve forecasting. Their successes have allowed us to have better warnings and more time to take cover before tornadoes hit. Their discoveries are saving lives.

As we enter a new century of weather, there are new questions to answer and more discoveries to be made. With more than 1,600 tornadoes hitting the United States in 2008, the year was second only to 2004 in the number of confirmed twisters.

How could this increase of tornadic activity be explained? Is it because of better reporting and simply a larger population available to witness the twisters? Is the increase because of an overheated atmosphere and the climate change of global warming?

Those questions weigh especially heavy on the minds of meteorologists in southwest Missouri. They observed the incredible winter tornado outbreak of 2008. In a 12-hour period, there were 62 tornado warnings and 161 severe weather reports. Twisters knocked out power and killed people along the Interstate 44 corridor.

The tornado tales in this book conclude with the May 2009 assault on Kirksville and north-central Missouri. However, it's safe to say that the last word on Show Me State twisters can never, ever be written. There are more tornadoes to come—and more words to be written about their awe-inspiring horror.

It is not unusual for the sun to be coming into view in the wake of a tornado.

Storm Strength

Likely F3

Number of Fatalities

At least 2

Time and Location

2:30 PM on February 27, 1876; St. Charles

1876: St. Charles Winter Murderer

Before a tornado hits, the wind may die down eerily—and the air can become very still. Or, sheets of rain, hail, and debris may blow sideways—and be punctuated by great bolts of blue and white lightning.

There is no "average tornado," but they do generally occur on the trailing edge of a towering thunderstorm. Hence, it is not uncommon for clear, sunlit skies to appear shortly after the tornado-packed storm performs its deadly deeds and passes. Such was the case in February of 1876 when a tornado hit the town of St. Charles on the banks of the Missouri River. Minutes after the winter tornado left the city in a crumpled heap of destruction, a bright sun came out to cast light upon the sorry mess left behind.

The *St. Charles Cosmos Monitor* newspaper described the storm as a terrible cloud column possessing the properties of "a steam blower locomotive engine, but magnified 100-fold." It roared through the city in less than a minute, leaving death and destruction every place it touched.

"After having followed the two main streets of the city to within three-hundred feet of the Wabash Bridge, the railroad bridge over the Missouri, the cyclone turned suddenly eastward, moved parallel to the bridge and then crossed it in the middle of its fourth span," wrote the reporter for the *Cosmos Monitor*.

"For a second, the cloud obscured the span, a flying roof soaring fifty feet above it, but in another instant the grand old bridge loomed out clear and sharp," the reporter added.

Roofs were not the only things seen flying over the St. Charles bridge. Some observers reported that a little child was seen flying over the span. In the end, at least two citizens were confirmed dead with many more injured. Other casualties accrued from what residents described as "the half-minute hurricane." Banks were damaged, as was the St. Charles County Courthouse. The famous Concert Hall next to the courthouse was damaged beyond repair.

St. Charles, the second oldest city west of the Mississippi, has had many famous visitors in its long history. For many years, state legislators visited the river town, because it served as the capital of Missouri for five years after statehood was declared in 1821.

Other noted visitors included Louis Blanchette in 1765, whose adventures in early America are chronicled in Menra Hopewell's *Legends of the Missouri and Mississippi*. The most famous visitors to St. Charles have to be Meriwether Lewis and William Clark, who arrived in 1804 near the beginning of their famous expedition. In the harsh light of that infamous tornado of 1876, much-appreciated visitors to St. Charles now are the folks who man its St. Louis National Weather Service Forecast Office.

Tornadoes have always been likened to locomotives, and in the weather disaster of 1880, a young Marshfield boy described that the twister looked like smoke belching from a locomotive.

Storm Strength

Likely F3

Number of Fatalities

At least 81

Time and Location

5:00 PM on April 18, 1880; Marshfield

1880: A STEAM ENGINE HITS MARSHFIELD

For many years, tornadoes have been compared to steam engines, runaway locomotives, and freight trains. Even before the Transcontinental Railroad crossed America's Great Plains in the 1860s, great twisters were likened to the great iron horse. Meteorologist and author J. P. Espy described a New England tornado in 1839 as having the auditory impact of the "rumbling of a thousand trains." The 1876 killer tornado in St. Charles was described as having the properties of "a steam blower locomotive" in a number of press accounts.

On April 18, 1880, a young boy gazed out his family's kitchen window in Marshfield, Missouri, as his mother was preparing a Sunday supper. He thought he saw a train. He saw what he described to his parents as heavy, dark smoke belching from the stacks of a great steam engine.

The youngster's father realized right away that the great plume in the distance did not originate from some "steam blower locomotive." His dad recognized immediately that it was a tornado and that the family needed to get out of the house quickly to find a sturdier structure for protection.

Fifty years after this tornado, W. D. Chitty, the boy who alerted his father to the approaching behemoth, gave an eyewitness account of the event to the local newspaper, the *Marshfield Mail*. He recalled how he had never before seen such a fit of fear take control of his father's face as on that fateful day.

The frantic father rushed young Chitty and his mother to Marshfield's strongest building for shelter, the downtown county courthouse. Inside, the wide-eyed son watched a man struggling outside the door in a futile effort to pull his wife into the building. The tornado was bearing down.

"The wind rose to a fiendish shriek as if all the demons of hell had been let loose upon doomed Marshfield," recalled W. D. Chitty. "From the shelter of the lobby, looking out the door, I saw part of the tin roof of the brick block turn away and fly into space as if some gigantic hand had ripped away a piece of paper from a writing pad. The air became thick with dust until breathing was difficult.

"Everybody prayed," Chitty added. "I prayed. Some prayed at the top of their lungs with a sort of frenzy. Someone shouted that it was the end of the world."

The young boy returned to the spot of his home after the furious funnel of wind disappeared on a trail to the northeast. Nothing remained of the home but a barren floor and shattered walls. Nearby came cries from those injured in both body and spirit.

Nature's great steam engine was replaced within a few hours by rescue trains built by man. The relief trains with doctors, nurses, and supplies arrived from neighboring towns. So much to tend to—more than eighty dead and two hundred injured. Of two hundred dwellings, not more than twenty were left standing.

Hopkins undoubtedly suffered from an F5 tornado in 1881 very much like this monster that hit Oklahoma decades later.

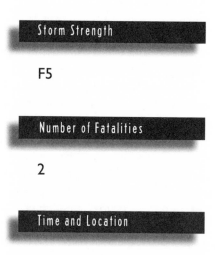

Storm Strength

F5

Number of Fatalities

2

Time and Location

3:00 PM on June 12, 1881; Hopkins and Nodaway County

Historians of extreme weather have long chronicled both the rare and the spectacular in the meteorologically moody Midwest. One such atmospheric terror event occurred in 1881 when a slew of hydra-headed tornadoes all combined to form one total monster.

This marriage from the heavens, conjoining the raging winds of hell, happened in northwest Missouri on a Sunday afternoon. Sparsely populated Nodaway County took the brunt of the calamity, which blew apart farmhouses and stables on a wide stretch.

Hundreds of cattle, horses, hogs, sheep, and a number of humans, perished in this odd storm. Nature's dark magic act, which involved combining several tornadoes into one big basilisk, caught a nation's attention.

Newspapers across the United States tried to explain how the scurrilous strands from the sky commingled to form one slithering serpent. What a blasphemy that the horrid act took place on a day of rest in a corner of "God's Country."

Although storms raged several days earlier to the west in Kansas, that June Sunday in Hopkins began inauspiciously. After dutifully attending church services and hearing the preachers' sermons, families in the rural enclave took some comfort on farmhouse porches after noon.

By 2 p.m., menacing clouds began to march on Hopkins, Pickering, and Maryville, the seat of Nodaway County. By 3 p.m., fierce tornadoes fell from the black cloud canopy and then began coupling.

The first victim of the long day of ravishing was the poor Lone Elm Schoolhouse, about six miles west of Hopkins. Meanwhile, other tornadoes were forming in Andrew, Gentry, and DeKalb counties. This was no day of rest in the skies of rural Missouri.

Although the Fujita Scale for measuring the strength of tornadoes did not exist at the time of the 1881 Hopkins twister, weather experts believe the tornado must have been an F5. An F5 is described as a twister that can carry entire homes for some distance. An F5 has winds in excess of 260 miles per hour.

Not much has happened in tiny Hopkins since the hydra-headed tornadoes of 1881. In 1933, an outlaw wanted for bank robbery and murder was gunned down in Hopkins in a bloody battle with the state highway patrol. Another big tornado hit on another Sunday of doom in 1952 and did major damage to the downtown.

So why has Hopkins been singled out for destruction from the skies? Why do twisters from the heavens rake poor Hopkins on the Lord's Day?

Some blame it all on Hopkins' most famous citizen, who believed in occult practices and telepathy with spirits. Born in 1867, Grant Wallace created art and writing that were proclaimed a sacrilege. His works appear in the study "The End is Near! Visions of Apocalypse, Millennium and Utopia."

Excelsior Brewery's ninety-foot smokestack was toppled by the 1890 cyclone. The Louis Obert and Lemp breweries also sustained damage.

Storm Strength

F2

Number of Fatalities

4

Time and Location

January 12, 1890; St. Louis

1890: St. Louis Winter Outbreak

Wild and wicked storms have long been fodder for the sensationalist press, and the yellow journalists of the late nineteenth century never saw a calamity or catastrophe that they didn't relish reporting.

Grisly details of nature's wrath filled the daily sheets emanating from the empires of William Randolph Hearst and Joseph Pulitzer. Both publishers employed "sob sisters," female reporters who were thought to be particularly adept at penning tragic tales to pull at the heartstrings.

Perhaps the best-known and most widely read news story of nature's destruction was that of Winifred Black, otherwise known as Annie Laurie. Her description of life lost in the 1900 hurricane and tidal wave in Galveston, Texas, is legendary. Black described rooting through the piles of debris and slime of a once beautiful city, and noted: "There are things that gripe the heart to see—a baby's shoe, for instance, a little red shoe, with a jaunty tasseled lace; a bit of a woman's dress and letters . . ."

Like the gulf city of Galveston, the river city of St. Louis dealt with the horror of what nature could dish out during the epic period of yellow journalism. And the journalists of the time dished out sensationalist prose covering the city's two traumatic encounters with tornadoes—first in 1890 and then again in 1896.

St. Louis was a dynamic, growing city in 1890. Its population leapt past 450,000, placing it in the top five U.S. cities. Its rail and river traffic made it one of the busiest crossroads of commerce in America. Some argued St. Louis should be the new U.S. capital. A prosperous middle class was building new neighborhoods out from the city's core. Homes and businesses were being built with the city's trademark red bricks. Those ruddy bricks became killers when the tornado of January 1890 blew into St. Louis.

Of course, the papers did not refer to the demon as a tornado. Instead, it was a murderous cyclone. "Thrilling Scene During the Passage of the Cyclone" screamed one news subhead under a verb-less, matter-of-fact, title head: "The Destruction In St. Louis."

After news leads about the horrible roar and the terrible wind, the body of the stories told of deaths caused by scalps torn off and skulls fractured. In most cases, the damage was done by bricks carried for blocks and blocks by the ferocious wind.

Men, women, and children were instantly killed. One story described the final breaths of Ida Weaver's boy, whose body was recovered by firemen.

St. Louis has always been known as a city of breweries and churches. It should come as no surprise, then, to learn that the cyclone of 1890 took out both such enterprises. The tall spire of the Emmanuel Church on Morgan Street was toppled, as was the ninety-foot smokestack of the Excelsior Brewery at 18th and Market streets.

Rated as the deadliest storm ever to hit St. Louis, the 1896 storm buried scores of residents under heaps of brick and timber.

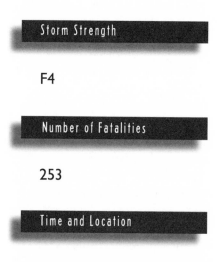

Storm Strength

F4

Number of Fatalities

253

Time and Location

6:30 PM on May 27, 1896; St. Louis

1896: St. Louis Ugly Tail Twister

Major American cities, for the most part, have been spared the ugly death tolls and destruction of direct hits on their downtowns by powerful tornadoes. However, both Kansas City and St. Louis are exceptions to this general rule of weather behavior.

Meteorologists explain the rarity of tornadoes striking the urban cores of major cities by noting the relatively few population centers within Tornado Alley. They also note that downtowns compose a very small target of real estate compared to the many square miles of rural flatlands which make up most twister-prone states of the Great Plains.

Metropolitan St. Louis has a tragic history of encounters with deadly squalls and funnels dropping from the sky, even though the great renowned river city sits several hundred miles from the widely accepted borders of what is termed Tornado Alley. Years in which the city of St. Louis felt the fatal sting of a tornado's fury include 1871, when 9 died; 1927, when 79 died; and 1959, when 21 were killed. However, the deadliest tornado of all occurred in 1896 when more than 135 died in St. Louis and another 118 died in the surrounding areas. East St. Louis, across the river, was hit especially hard.

Press accounts have the tornado starting near the "Insane Asylum" on Arsenal Street, then crushing areas such as Lafayette Park and Soulard on the city's south side. The hurricane then tossed boats around like toys on the Mississippi, before taking out the Illinois approach to the Eads Bridge and bringing many lives to an end in East St. Louis.

Although the tornado is called a cyclone and a hurricane in the press accounts, it would be more accurate to describe it as Godzilla. Journalists of the time wrote as if it were a living monster, complete with body and tail, swinging its frightful appendage around with deadly purpose.

"About the time it was directly over the Scullin power house the tail came along, swept under, and with a roar that was heard for blocks, mixed motors, engines cars, machinery and men in a mass of matter," wrote one frenzied reporter.

"Then the tail swung over to the South Side race track, completely licked it off the face of the earth, and the great body, flashing lightning and breathing thunder, moved swiftly to the northeast . . . ," he continued.

More words have been written about the 1896 killer Godzilla that attacked St. Louis than any other tornadic storm to hit the United States. Many of those words were compiled days after the storm in an "instant book" printed by Cyclone Publishing. Titled *The Great Cyclone*, the book tells how St. Louis was bruised and blistered by that ugly twister tail. A collection of "thrilling and pathetic incidents" from the 1896 cataclysm, the book was reprinted by Southern Illinois University in 1997.

Kirksville-area residents survey the sparse remains of a section of town shattered by the 1899 suppertime killer.

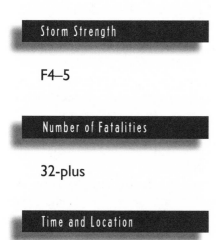

Storm Strength

F4–5

Number of Fatalities

32-plus

Time and Location

6:00 PM on April 27, 1899; Kirksville

1899: Kirksville Killer of the Young

Tornadoes are not merely deadly. They can be graphic and gruesome in their serial slaughter. The merciless killer which stalked Kirksville in April 1899 crushed bodies, ripped off human limbs, and tore off scalps. Tornadoes are indiscriminate in their selection of victims. The worst of them take out the very young and the very old—and all those in between. In the worst storm ever to hit Kirksville, located in north-central Missouri, the cruel winds exacted an especially heavy toll on the town's young.

More than thirty-two people lost their lives that wicked evening, and hundreds more were injured. According to newspaper accounts of the April 27 storm, the tornado began twelve miles southwest of Kirksville near Troy Mills. The rotating killer churned through the town of Kirksville and then headed up past the Iowa border, where it reportedly deposited a number of the belongings of Kirksville citizens.

The *Kirksville Weekly Graphic* and other papers in Adair County later printed storm summary stories with differing details. One thing they all agreed on—this storm's mayhem was multiplied by the number of fires that broke out among the shattered homes in its aftermath.

Perhaps some of these fires resulted from overturned cooking stoves. The tornado arrived at suppertime, and many of the casualties were in the kitchens of Kirksville homes. The burning home debris cremated a number of victims who were robbed of a proper memorial service and burial. Among those in Kirksville who had their supper so rudely interrupted were the students of the American School of Osteopathy, the State Normal School, and McWard's Seminary. A list of casualties included some of the students as their boarding houses were leveled.

According to the 1901 *Encyclopedia of the History of Missouri*, a girl of sixteen was discovered dead with a two-by-four strut thrust through her body. Another lifeless child with a tree limb through the neck was removed from a mound of ruins. An infant was carried by the wind and dropped in a field with no serious injury.

At least forty-five citizens were lost to the wind-driven grim reaper, which made a track about four blocks in width through the city. Some reports have a second tornado, "an inky black cloud" traveling over the city about twenty minutes after the first angry visitor.

The 1899 tornado was especially hard on the young, but some speculate that a similar twister today would take out even more young folks. This is because of the presence of Truman State University. Several of its residence halls would have been in the direct path of the 1899 killer.

In 1999, one hundred years after the worst disaster to ever hit Kirksville, a historic exhibit was put together on the Truman campus to remind residents of nature's wrath a century ago.

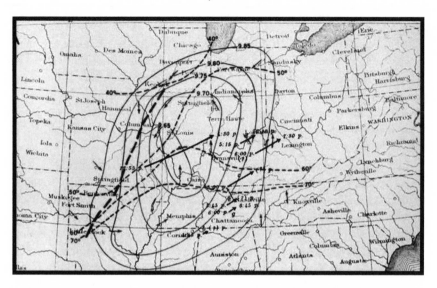

America's greatest tornado disaster of all time began near Ellington, Missouri, and tracked along a line northeast through Illinois to Indiana.

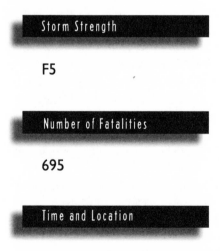

Storm Strength

F5

Number of Fatalities

695

Time and Location

1:00 PM on March 18, 1925; Ellington

1925: Ellington-Born Tri-State Tornado Disaster

Never has a single tornado caused as much grief and prompted as many tears as the legendary Tri-State Tornado of 1925. It changed human lives forever in portions of southern Missouri, Illinois, and Indiana.

The Tri-State horror was one of the longest, fastest, and widest to spindle down to earth. Peter Felnor in his twister tome *The Tri-State Tornado: The Story of America's Greatest Tornado Disaster*, recalls how some Illinois towns were simply scrubbed from the terrain, terminated, never to be seen or heard from again.

The tornado, which killed 234 of the citizens of Murphysboro, Illinois, and destroyed 40 percent of that town, had its humble beginnings in a pasture near Ellington, Missouri. Although it is often called the "Great Southern Illinois Tornado," the twister left its mark on Reynolds, Iron, Madison, Bollinger, Cape Girardeau, and Perry counties in Missouri before making the jump across the Mississippi River.

Even at its first kiss of the ground northwest of Ellington, the descending funnel was a killer, ending the life of a humble farmer. At times, the dark funnel became extremely wide—a plowing cloud of destruction—snapping trees, lifting up farmhouses, and leveling schools.

The storm's downbursts and fierce tornadic winds were especially hard on Annapolis and the tiny mining town of Leadanna. More than seventy-five were injured in the area of Iron County and at least two lost their lives.

After punishing the small hamlets of Missouri's famed Lead Belt, the intense storm traveled through the hills south of Fredericktown. The southeast Ozark hills did nothing to diminish the squall's energy. Once it cleared hill country and sped out onto farmland in Bollinger and Perry counties, the vortex began to roll up its remarkable death toll.

Small towns with odd names like Lixville, Biehle, and Frohna were caught unaware and simply crushed. The tornado began near Ellington around 1 p.m., so it was in time for school when it reached these towns. A child was killed in a school north of Altenburg and thirty-two more were injured in two Bollinger County schools.

The tornado then tracked north of Tower Rock, the infamous limestone outcropping in the Mississippi River. If the storm had stopped north of the big rock—its funnel sucked back into the black sky for good—it would still have been recorded as one of nature's worst. Thirteen Missourians were left dead with scores injured.

However, the Show Me State was just the beginning for the Tri-State Tornado. Illinois and Indiana were destined to see the worst of the tornado. When it completed its 219-mile path, 695 lost their lives and more than 2,000 were injured. Three and a half hours after taking out a Missouri farmer near Ellington, the tornado disappeared in skies near Princeton, Indiana.

Webster Groves is sometimes credited as the starting point for the great twister of 1927, but it did its worst damage in St. Louis, where rows of buildings were demolished.

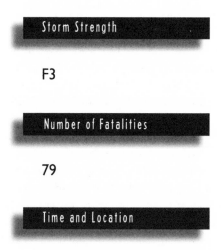

Storm Strength

F3

Number of Fatalities

79

Time and Location

12:50 PM on September 29, 1927; St. Louis

1927: Twister Birthed in Webster Groves

Webster Groves and its sister city, Kirkwood, both inner-ring suburbs of St. Louis, are no strangers to storms rolling in from the west with fierce lightning and tornadic force.

Both towns take pride in their giant trees which all sport thick, leafy canopies. Both towns suffer massive losses when sweeping winds and storm downbursts topple the giants across rails, roofs, and roadways.

Both towns take exceptional pride in their official designations as "tree cities," and both have argued for decades over which one is the true "Queen of the Suburbs" of greater St. Louis. If, indeed, Webster Groves be that queen, then she birthed a wild child in late September 1927.

On the 29th of that month a funnel cloud was sighted in south Webster Groves. The black whirlwind began to roil, uncoil, and descend in the town's Old Orchard district and then headed up Big Bend Road. The twister touched the ground in Maplewood and then had its way with the beautiful Forest Park of St. Louis.

The storm took down trees in the east part of Forest Park, took a slice out of the Central West End of St. Louis, and headed to downtown and the riverfront. In the city's core, its path widened from 100 to 1,800 feet and the twister began blowing entire buildings away.

Archived images from the old *St. Louis Globe-Democrat* provide the best documentation of the incredible destruction of the super twister.

Rows of multi-story buildings had their top floors decapitated. Many one-story residences had their insides sucked to the heavens. They were left as shells with wall facades teetering from the loss of any support.

Although the twister spent less than five minutes of its grim span in St. Louis, it shredded six square miles of heavily populated neighborhoods. Many people were trapped in the ruins of the old Central High School, where about 1,500 students were attending afternoon classes.

Other city schools lost their roofs, steeples crashed down from churches, cars were overturned, steel girders were thrown around like tinker toys, and humans flew without wings. People caught outdoors, who failed to react and to assume a prone position, were launched skyward.

More than 70 souls lost the flame of life that September day, and about 550 were injured. *Globe-Democrat* photographs from the day of disaster include many shots of Salvation Army workers digging through the rubble and providing aid.

The merciless twister proceeded on to less-populated areas in Illinois but continued its massive destruction. National Weather Service records indicate the storm was the second costliest tornado in U.S. history. What a devil was delivered by the "Queen of the Suburbs" on that oppressive fall day in September of 1927.

Poplar Bluff residents have always called their town "Best City in Southeast Missouri," but it suffered a near-lethal blow with the twister of 1927.

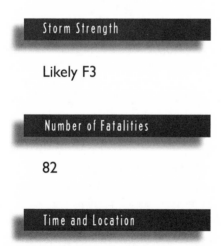

Storm Strength

Likely F3

Number of Fatalities

82

Time and Location

3:17 PM on May 9, 1927; Poplar Bluff

1927: Poplar Bluff Teachers v. Tornado

Folks in Poplar Bluff take pride in calling their town the "Best City in Southeast Missouri." The town claims unique and interesting history to back up its proclamations of pride. Upon reading the various accounts of the great tornado of 1927, it's hard not make another proclamation: "Let us now praise the caring legacy of the teachers of Poplar Bluff."

For in the great biblioclasm which battered the city in May 1927, Poplar Bluff schoolteachers kept their heads while others were losing theirs—figuratively and literally. The teachers kept their young charges in the safety of the school building—just as the approach of a monster cyclone was coinciding with the bell signaling the end of another day at school.

Monday, May 9, 1927, may have seemed like just another school day in Poplar Bluff, but it was not. Skies were threatening by early afternoon, and at 3:15 p.m.—about the time kids should be walking home from school—the skies made good on their threats.

The tornado killed ten persons southwest of Poplar Bluff before it drove its head of deadly steam into town. Soon bricks, timber, and steel joined in the raucous rotation—lethal flying bullets that were responsible for many of the eighty-two deaths in the city on the Black River.

The storm drew national attention for its ferocity, and in St. Louis, the old *Globe-Democrat* noted that seven hundred children from local schools could have been walking home through the business district, which was directly in the giant twister's path. "The majority of them leave their schools and go home by way of the business district," noted the daily *St. Louis Globe-Democrat*. "But the tornado found them safely under the care of their teachers."

Poplar Bluff school buildings withstood the blast, but businesses and the courthouse were a wreck in less than ninety seconds. The New Melbourne Hotel collapsed and crushed eighteen residents to death. Fires erupted in some fallen structures, and poor souls that survived the storm were subsequently burned to death.

The Associated Press reported that the destruction of Poplar Bluff was worse than the carnage in the 1925 Tri-State Tornado in Murphysboro, Illinois. Such news stories inspired relief workers to come to the town by train to help with the cleanup. Tents, cots, and bedding were donated to homeless families.

The headquarters of the *Daily Republican* of Poplar Bluff was in ruins and its typesetting equipment in tatters. A bulletin was reportedly printed by hand on an old job press. "Are Poplar Bluffians down hearted?" asked the *Daily Republican*. "Are they disgusted with the efforts to build the best city . . . ? The answer is found on every hand—a thousand times NO. Poplar Bluff will be rebuilt, bigger and better than ever!"

Most tornadoes have life cycles that begin and end in unpopulated, rural areas where their impact is minimal. However, if they hit urban areas they can do irreparable damage to landmarks that have endured for years.

Storm Strength

Likely F3

Number of Fatalities

21

Time and Location

6:56 PM on May 21, 1949; Cape Girardeau

1949: Cape Girardeau Red Cross v. Tornado

The cape for which the city of Cape Girardeau is named has regrettably vanished. The great, solid rock on the Missouri side of the unpredictable Mississippi River is long gone. An argument could ensue on the foolhardiness of not granting this rock some respect—the same reverence accorded to another rock in the vicinity of Plymouth, Massachusetts. That, however, would be futile. Missouri's rock landmark was long ago sacrificed to the rail needs of freight trains running south along the waterfront.

Another Cape Girardeau landmark disappeared forever on the evening of Saturday, May 21, 1949. This time, a manmade landmark was lost. It was pulverized by nature's own version of a runaway freight train. A war-like tornado came storming into Cape, and in a matter of seconds huge pieces of the Airline Restaurant and Lounge were lifted into the ether. Most of this well-known Cape Girardeau restaurant was leveled into a pile of useless debris. More outrageous than the loss of the landmark restaurant and lounge was the tragic loss of life in the path of the twister.

In all, the twister claimed 21 lives, and more than 100 others were injured. Home subdivisions on the east side of Highway 61 and north of Southeast Missouri State University endured the worst of the storm. More than 220 homes and businesses were declared beyond repair, and another 250 suffered wind damage.

The only incident more deadly in Cape than the May 21, 1949, tornado was the Civil War Battle of Cape Girardeau which took place on April 26, 1863. Union and Confederate armies clashed in a dramatic, four-hour artillery barrage. On that fateful day in Cape, thirty Confederates of the South and twenty-three Union soldiers were marked for the grave.

Hostilities in the war between the states ended officially about two years after the Cape battle. Forces of the Confederacy surrendered on April 9, 1865. Skirmishes continued west of the Mississippi River, but finally ceased by the end of May in 1865.

As all Missourians from Cape to Kirksville to Kansas City well know, the hostilities in the heavens never completely cease. Clashes between the moist air masses of the south and the weather fronts from the north and west are a threat every month of the year. Climatologists know the uncivil wars in the skies over the Midwest will never be quieted by a truce.

In May of 1949, the stage was set for a heavenly battle over southeast Missouri when air masses collided and storms erupted. Nature's heavy artillery was unleashed when the battle turned tornadic, and the vortex roared through Cape Girardeau.

Afterward, Red Cross workers, who came to the rescue from as far as St. Louis, said old Cape looked like a war zone. Well, it was a war zone.

Tornadoes that display multi-vortex characteristics, such as those that hit the south Kansas City area in 1957, can prove especially deadly.

Storm Strength

F5

Number of Fatalities

44

Time and Location

6:15 PM on May 20, 1957; Kansas City and Pleasant Hill

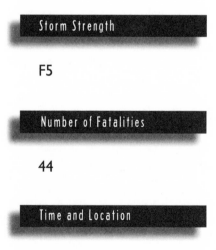

1957: KANSAS CITY RUSKIN HEIGHTS DISASTER

A few especially powerful tornadic events are so awesome, so frightening that they no longer seem a progeny of nature. Rather, the angry sky vortexes seem more like visitors from outer space—aliens bringing forth a nightmare such as H. G. Wells conceived in *War of the Worlds*.

In the unprecedented Kansas-Missouri tornado outbreak of May 1957, eyewitnesses reported a weird spectacle of tentacles dropping down from cloudbanks, bouncing off the befuddled earth in a bizarre dance, and then merging together in a monster of mammoth proportions. Funnels were fulminating in western Kansas skies several hours before the great conflagration. The rotating wind spirals began dropping to earth as they neared the Missouri border.

One multi-tornado, which brought about the most horrendous destruction from this macabre dance, varied in width from just a couple of city blocks to one-half mile. It sped into the southeast suburbs of Kansas City at about forty miles per hour.

The Kansas City suburb of Ruskin Heights was hit just before 8 p.m. on that miserable evening of Monday, May 20, 1957. According to the U.S. Weather Service, the big one first ripped into the shopping center at 111th Street and Blue Ridge Boulevard on the Kansas City area's south side. It then paid an unwelcome visit to Ruskin Heights High School. High school administrators had conducted a baccalaureate service on Sunday. A graduation was scheduled for Tuesday evening, but on Monday night the high school blew away.

Ruskin Heights members of the Class of 1957 still wonder how many would have died had commencement taken place on Monday. In any case, at least thirty-nine residents of the area did die from the storm's wrath and more than five hundred were injured. One wall left standing at the high school gym lost letters on its signage, and "Ruskin" was transformed into R-U-I-N.

Ruin and rubble were everywhere in Ruskin. Many families rode out the storm piled together in basements. As debris began to fill the air, other residents hit the road out of town in their cars—not always such a good idea. The town's water tower actually was hit by an airborne automobile.

In the storm's aftermath, confused survivors tried to piece together what had happened to them. Homes were shredded; trees were ripped apart; the acrid smell of electrical ozone filled the air, which was not yet clear of the power line flotsam from the funnel's finalé.

The great Ruskin Heights Tornado is now remembered with a monument where memorial services periodically take place. The sad event also is recalled in the pages of several books, including Carolyn Brewer's *Caught in the Path: A Tornado's Fury, a Community's Rebirth*. She gives her recollections as a child survivor and describes the sheer horror of being assaulted by a multiple-vortex, F5 tornado.

The Dark Side, where jazz and drinks flowed nightly, took a hit from the Gaslight Square tornado of 1957 along with other hot spots like Smokey Joe's Grecian Terrace.

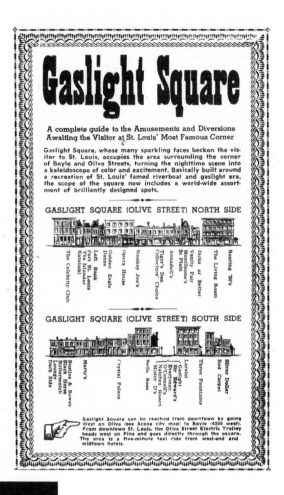

Gaslight Square

A complete guide to the Amusements and Diversions Awaiting the Visitor at St. Louis' Most Famous Corner

Gaslight Square, whose many sparkling faces beckon the visitor to St. Louis, occupies the area surrounding the corner of Boyle and Olive Streets, turning the nighttime scene into a kaleidoscope of color and excitement. Basically built around a recreation of St. Louis' famed riverboat and gaslight era, the scope of the square now includes a world-wide assortment of brilliantly designed spots.

GASLIGHT SQUARE (OLIVE STREET) NORTH SIDE

The Celebrity Club · Port St. Louis The Islander Kokobuki · Left Bank · Golden Eagle Danza · Opera House · Smokey Joe's · Tiger's Den Collectors' Choice · Annadell's · Vanity Fair Montilione's 2c Plain · Jacks or Better · The Living Room · Roaring '20's

GASLIGHT SQUARE (OLIVE STREET) SOUTH SIDE

Bustles & Bowes Black Horse Butterscotch Lounge Dark Side · Mardy's · Crystal Palace · Rolls Ross · Gaslight Everyman O'Connell's Natchez Queen Mister D's · Loreled Sir Edward's · Three Fountains · Silver Dollar Red Carpet

Gaslight Square can be reached from downtown by going West on Olive (see Scene city map) to Boyle (4300 west). From downtown St. Louis, the Olive Street Electric Trolley heads west on Pine and goes directly through the square. The area is a five-minute taxi ride from west-end and midtown hotels.

Storm Strength

F4

Number of Fatalities

21

Time and Location

1:10 AM on February 10, 1959; St. Louis

1959: Bully of Gaslight Square

Gaslight Square in St. Louis was once the hippest place to be in the world, at least according to all those with fond memories of the long-lost entertainment district of the 1950s. Barbra Streisand, Lenny Bruce, Tommy Smothers, Judy Collins, and groups like Peter, Paul & Mary found Gaslight Square to be a suitable venue for their nationally recognized talents. For St. Louisans, it was a must-see place—and a place to be seen.

At the intersection of Olive and Boyle, the Square's evening lights reflected on bars, nightclubs, go-go joints, restaurants, offbeat stores, and myriad antique shops. Those lights also illuminated a piece of Arch City history that has never dimmed in the minds of those who experienced it socially and culturally.

So what happened to Gaslight Square? What happened to the Greenwich Village of St. Louis? It's not like Gaslight was squeezed out by competitors, by other popular corners of entertainment in the city.

Some blame the loss on the creep of crime, at first muggings and petty thefts, and then a highly publicized murder. Others blame the demise of Gaslight on a big bully that came to town on an unusually warm evening in February—the tornado of 1959. It may not have been the end, but it was the beginning of the end.

This freak tornado did not just do dirty to Gaslight Square. For most St. Louisans, the most visible results of the tornado included the loss of parts of the roof of the old Arena, home to St. Louis Hawks basketball. Another major casualty was the Channel 2 TV antenna tower, which was south of Oakland Avenue near the Arena.

More tragic were the twenty dead and three hundred injured in St. Louis from the storm that struck at 2 a.m. Gaslight Square, home to the Crystal Palace, the Dark Side, and the Laughing Buddha, took a direct hit.

For those St. Louisans with a Reverend Pat Robertson frame of mind, the Gaslight Square tornado may have symbolized the justice of the Lord. After all, the Square was a gathering area for the decadent, a hangout for drinking, smoking, dancing, and carousing into the wee hours.

However, according to St. Louis writer Tom Crone's excellent oral history *Gaslight Square*, at least one resident was up reading the good book as the tornado hit. That resident was "Smokey" Joe Cunningham, a popular outfielder for the baseball Cardinals, who lived above a Square restaurant.

"If you ever go through a hurricane or a tornado like that, you never forget those things," Cunningham told Crone. "I remember the next day, this guy from the TV station asked me what I was doing and I said, 'to be honest, I was reading the Bible.' I got kidded a lot about that, that story got all over. . . . I'm not ashamed to say it. I was reading the Bible."

Tornadoes in the Midwest occur primarily in the spring months, but some of the deadliest are spawned in winter.

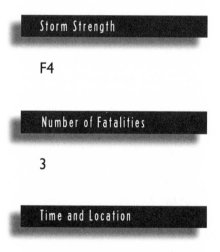

Storm Strength

F4

Number of Fatalities

3

Time and Location

6:55 PM on January 24, 1967; St. Louis

1967: St. Louis Winter Twister

A widely accepted axiom of those who reside in the land of the Gateway Arch goes like this: "If you don't like the weather in St. Louis, just wait a minute." Skies, temperatures, humidity, and wind direction are subject to abrupt, zig-zag changes without much notice in St. Louis.

When storm fronts barrel through the region and the wind shifts, it's not unusual for temperatures to fall like a rock. In the dark of winter, rain will transform into noisy ice pellets, then to sleet, then to heavy wet snow, and then, finally, to wispy angel dust.

On January 24, 1967, the infamous St. Louis County tornado struck, and in so doing swept away the milder air from a different season. Within hours after the surprise winter tornado, continuing thunderstorms produced cold rain, freezing rain, sleet, and snow.

The snow which followed the tornado outbreak brought blizzard conditions to much of the Midwest. South Wisconsin and the Chicago area also dealt with freak tornadoes and then were carpeted by a thick blanket of about two feet of snow.

St. Louis County's unusual winter tornado was one of fourteen spawned in the Midwest. The winter whirler covered a path from the Chesterfield area, past Creve Coeur Lake, and up to the great confluence of the Mississippi and Missouri rivers. It then quickly dissipated as it crossed into Illinois.

The National Weather Service, known officially in 1967 as the Weather Bureau, lost its radar and its phone service for a time when the twister passed just south of its office at the airport at Lambert Field.

Some time after the winter storm, the weather agency rated the tornado as F4 on the Fujita Tornado Ranking Scale. Three deaths in the area were reported, with 216 injuries. Destroyed homes were tallied at 168 with another 258 suffering major damage. An estimate for the destruction by the twister was placed at $15 million.

The mighty tornado, which was on the ground for just about thirty-five minutes, affirms the old adage about St. Louis weather changing in just a matter of moments. The winter storm also blew away the mythology that tornadoes do not develop in those cooler months when daylight is in short supply.

Tornadoes in the Midwest do occur mostly in the spring months. In the decades since 1950, however, many of the worst twisters have occurred in winter. A study by meteorologists with the National Severe Storms Forecast Center in Kansas City has noted: "Long track winter outbreak tornadoes account for a greater percentage of deaths than the long-track spring outbreak tornadoes."

Is global warming making winter tornadoes worse? Weather experts are sure of one thing: Tornado-spawning storms move faster in winter. That leaves much less time for warning folks to get out of harm's way.

Fig 30. ATS-III Photo. 1511 GMT. April 3. 1974

Weather Service satellite photos on April 3, 1974, show the incredible stormfront that passed through St. Louis with tornadic-like force before spawning twisters farther east.

Storm Strength

F5

Number of Fatalities

30

Time and Location

2:08 PM on April 1–3, 1974; Missouri, Illinois, Michigan, Ohio, and Indiana

1974: Super Tornado Outbreak

Often described as the "Super Tornado Outbreak of 1974," the jumbo storm complex of early April that year generated a record 148 twisters—a natural disaster affecting 13 states. As an article in a 2007 issue of *Popular Mechanics* magazine noted, the incredible April tornado outbreak constituted "the seventh of our 10 worst disasters of the last 101 years."

This backbreaking weather system revved up when a front pushed eastward roughly from south of St. Louis, through Bloomington, Illinois, to the Great Lakes. It brought tornadic-like winds, downpours, and large hail to St. Louis, although there seems to be no reported actual funnel clouds in the area.

Still, the mega-storm of last century deserves a place in any complete chronicle of fantastic weather events of the Missouri region. Why?

Because the storm front had much of its genesis in St. Louis. Many longtime residents recall the swift-moving storm and its green skies. They also remember the downburst winds and great balls of hail. Once the squall line passed through St. Louis, it began dropping tornadoes east of the Mississippi River.

According to *Popular Mechanics*, National Weather Service forecasters were using primitive 1950s-era radar at the time. Even so, forecasters could tell something ugly was brewing over the central United States. They issued 28 severe storm watches and 150 tornado warnings.

The squalls towered more than eleven miles high and grew into a frightening line more than twenty-five hundred miles long. The squalls moved an average of fifty miles per hour, although they were clocked moving through St. Louis at sixty miles per hour.

Once the front passed over St. Louis, killer tornadoes began wracking Illinois. A major piece of luck was that the tornadoes did not form over any major urban areas. Southern Indiana and northern Kentucky were hard hit, but the worst destruction of all occurred when the skies became a dark mass of twisting chaos over southwest Ohio.

The deadliest storm of all during the April 3 tornado outbreak occurred about 4:30 p.m. in Xenia, Ohio. Poor Xenia lacked a siren warning system, so most of its residents had no idea what was about to come their way. An eyewitness saw two tornadoes, almost in competition with each other, until they joined together in one huge column with rotating winds at 318 miles per hour.

A Xenia native, who talked about the historic storm years later with an Associated Press reporter, recalled: "I saw bedroom doors slamming against the wall before flying off the hinges. The roof ripped off, and the walls around us crumbled. Between my sobs, I could hear my dad praying for our protection."

A lot of praying was going on in the Midwest in early April 1974. Some of that praying began in St. Louis.

An F4 tornado, such as this super vortex in Oklahoma, struck the Springfield area of Missouri on Thanksgiving weekend in 1991.

Storm Strength

F4

Number of Fatalities

2

Time and Location

6:00 PM on November 29, 1991; Springfield

1991: Springfield Holiday Horror

The southwest Missouri cities of Joplin, Branson, and Springfield frame a sort of axis of evil when it comes to birthing ugly Rosemary's Baby tornadoes in the state. Perhaps it would be more apt to describe this axis as a tornadic triangle which these Missouri cities form. That's right. Call it the "Missouri Tornado Triangle," where the lives of men, women, and children are in peril when towering thunderheads build in nearby Arkansas and Oklahoma—then blow into southwest Missouri. Homes, businesses, schools, cars, trucks, and humans can often disappear in this tornado triangle when the Devils of Weather are frowning.

The Thanksgiving weekend tornado of 1991 devastated huge areas of the triangle and cast a pall on the Christmas plans of residents. The Branson and Springfield areas are known for doing their Christmases big. When the late fall tornado of 1991 hit the region, many Christmas plans had to be put on hold.

Springfield's Jim and Carolyn Welton intended to put up all their Christmas decorations on the weekend after Thanksgiving. Instead, they were left sifting through the remains of their shattered home.

"What a way to have an open house," Carolyn Welton told reporter Joan Little with the *St. Louis Post-Dispatch*, as she picked through the mess left in her roofless home. "We're here. That's the main thing."

Rescue volunteers on that unforgettable Thanksgiving weekend had a tough time reaching survivors buried under clutter left by Friday evening's twister. Several were found dead. More than sixty were injured. At least two hundred homes were damaged by the twister which swept from Nixa to the north subdivisions of Springfield. Among the lives snuffed out by the storm was that of Samuel Maranto, a retired executive from St. Louis. Maranto, who wrote a tennis column for the *Springfield News-Leader*, died when the house collapsed on him and his wife. She barely escaped death.

An Associated Press news story described the Thanksgiving weekend mayhem as a "rare autumn twister." However, twisters strike anytime in Missouri's Tornado Triangle. And, as with the original Bermuda Triangle, some of the terrible incidents in these cataclysms seem almost extraterrestrial, paranormal, beyond the normal laws of physics.

Perhaps one of the many oddities of the 1991 storm involved the way its destructive winds bore down on some of the most expensive real estate in the Springfield area. They were the kind of residences that would have been festooned for the season with colored lights, reindeer, and Santas.

Instead, the expensive homes were smashed to bits. Flattened Cadillacs and overturned BMWs littered front yards, where jolly elves and laughing Santas should have loitered under twinkling lights.

New mobile technology makes it tempting to photograph and take digital video of funnel clouds and tornadoes, but there is an obvious risk in failing to seek shelter when a tornadic storm is bearing down.

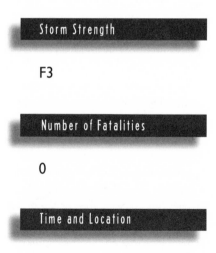

Storm Strength

F3

Number of Fatalities

0

Time and Location

12:00 PM on July 4, 1995; Moberly

1995: MOBERLY'S JULY 4TH TORNADO FIREWORKS

Folks with Moberly's Chamber of Commerce fondly refer to their town as the "Magic City," an accolade that harkens back to the Missouri city's founding in the 1870s. When the early railroad companies brought an important rail connection through the area about that time, Moberly sprang up upon the quiet prairie "as if by magic." Some decades later, it was not magic that sprang upon the prairie on a most memorable Independence Day.

Instead, on July 4, 1995, a powerful tornado hit the prairie ground and ripped into downtown Moberly. The proud town, halfway between Macon and Columbia on Highway 63, lost a portion of its downtown and a bit of its magic that fateful day.

The Moberly tornado has been the subject of scrutiny by meteorologists. A storm study by Pete Browning, John F. Weaver, and Bernadette Connell notes the exceptional circumstances of the Moberly tornado. A normally quiet summer pattern was intruded on by an intense jet stream.

There's no magic or superstition in the weather study about the Moberly event, but there are a lot of terms that may seem like hocus-pocus to the layperson. For example, there are references to "vorticity" and the "synoptic-scale upward motion" and "a quasi-stationary surface front."

For folks on the ground having picnics around Moberly, it was all about a holiday tornado. Many residents were outside barbecuing when the twister hit. For that reason, the July 4th tornado in Moberly may be one of the most photographed and videotaped funnels in the history of human encounters with tornadoes.

The photographs, which weather scientists have studied to understand the Moberly monster, were all taken from cameras aloft in outer space. This satellite imagery shows water vapor, a cold front, air outflows and three storm cells in Missouri on the day the vortex hit Moberly. Browning, Weaver, and Connell's expert study notes that when the middle storm in Missouri began to wind down, the storms to its north and south seemed to draw out its energy. Both storms then produced tornadoes.

Sequential satellite imagery shows the evolution of these storms. Study of such imagery helps with forecasting severe weather. The experts concluded from their study that even small interactions among storms, within a short timescale, can cause sudden tornado development, as if by magic.

Of course, the mysterious events in the sky on July 4, 1995, robbed some of the luster from Missouri's "Magic City." The business district was heavily damaged, and Moberly's downtown was Ground Zero and was pummeled.

The human toll could have been dramatic, if people had been working downtown. So, perhaps it is magical that Moberly's big tornado came to visit on a holiday, Independence Day.

Satellite photographs of nature's worst weather events reveal the intensity of massive storm systems.

Storm Strength

F3

Number of Fatalities

8

Time and Location

4:00–5:00 PM on May 4, 2003; Pierce City and the Ozarks

2003: Pierce City's Day of Devastation

Reporters at the daily *Springfield News-Leader* in southwest Missouri stay plenty busy during tornado season, and there's always the temptation to ask: When is it not tornado season in the Missouri Ozarks? Well, it's always tornado season, but the cruel skies are especially active from late March through June.

The Springfield daily's newspaper reporters were especially busy in May 2003, when raging twisters again plastered the paper's circulation area. The towns of Battlefield, Verona, Marionville, Billings, and Clever were hit hard. By far, Pierce City suffered the very worst of what nature had to offer in the spring of 2003.

Pierce City was slammed May 4 on a warm Sunday evening when the town endured its worst nightmare. About 90 percent of the historic downtown business district was wiped out. Perhaps the most tragic story in the Pierce City disaster involved residents who desperately took refuge in the National Guard Armory.

The Armory was supposed to be the town's storm shelter, but it collapsed from the raging winds. A dozen people were injured when the building failed, and one died from wounds received. The twister that took out Pierce City also destroyed farms and homes, but it was just one spring tornado of many that wracked the United States from April 30 through May 10.

More than four hundred tornadoes spun paths of destruction in nineteen states, one of the largest outbreaks in U.S. history. Southwest Missouri was among the hardest hit areas nationwide.

"There have been worse tornadoes that have struck the region, but it's been more years than anybody can remember that we've received this number of tornadoes," declared the Weather Service's Steve Runnells in an interview with the *News-Leader*.

Reporters with Springfield's paper found themselves in Pierce City for weeks after the mighty wind that brought the town to its knees. Just the task of cleaning up all the debris took months. The effort took place amidst signs reading, "Keep Pierce City Alive," taped to donation pails posted around the battered town.

Landfills outside of Pierce City piled up with twister refuse. Other things that piled up were the bills for insurance companies. Nationally, the spate of tornadoes had a price tag of $1.55 billion, according to the *News-Leader*. In Missouri, the costs climbed to $400 million.

A welcome and novel tale in the *News-Leader* appeared in July when the paper covered efforts to restore mangled forestland. The Pierce City area lost 2,193 wooded acres to the storm. Young folks pitched in to plant red cedars and eastern white pine. "Trees that did survive the twister resembled the aftermath of a five-year-old grabbing mom's scissors and giving himself a haircut," observed Jeff Arnold, a *News-Leader* reporter.

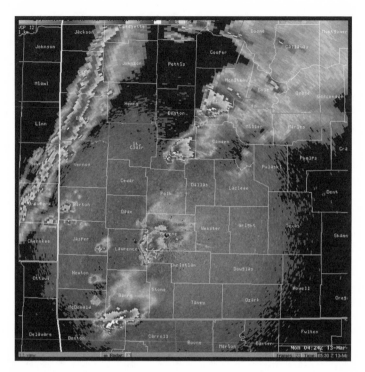

Severe storm outbreaks precede a well-organized front bearing down on Western Missouri.

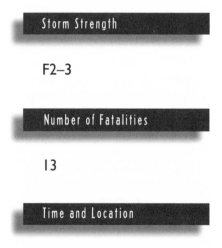

Storm Strength

F2–3

Number of Fatalities

13

Time and Location

10:00 PM on March 12, 2006; Lawerence County

2006: Ozark "Naders" from the Heavens

In the Ozark hill country of southern Missouri, Internet bloggers bring a certain folksiness to any discussion of the latest "naders" to drop down from scary skies— skies the color of "exorcist puke." Think pea green.

Blogging in the boonies about "hail bombs" and "juice bolts" provides a unique Ozark flavor to meteorological discussions. Bloggers in the vicinity of Branson's entertainment row, which the Baldknobbers call home, will talk about driving "like a bat out of the hottest part of hell" to escape "a sucker [an ugly nader] going full tilt and wrapped all up in a rain shield."

During the period of March 9 to March 13 in 2006, more than 106 "suckers going full tilt" were recorded in the central United States. Nothing funny about this terrible onslaught! The slew of twisters resulted in thirteen deaths and a bill for damages in excess of $1 billion. March 12 was the date for the worst destruction in towns south of Springfield, Missouri, when a series of "naders" reduced houses to rubble and hurled mobile homes into gulleys and across thoroughfares such as U.S. Highway 60.

In the age of the Internet, no one using the Web should have been surprised by the outbreak of "naders," particularly those bloggers who make a point of keeping up with weather. Four days out, the Storm Prediction Center in Norman, Oklahoma, was reporting a combination of moisture and temperatures to set the stage for an atmospheric eruption. Those observations were followed by a weather map with Missouri in the crosshairs of a supercell outbreak.

The warnings were posted. Nevertheless, there were surprises. Matt Suter was certainly shocked when the "exorcist puke" colored skies bore a deadly brew of rain, hail, and wind. That's because the Fordland, Missouri, teenager was blown through the air more than thirteen hundred feet by the "nader" that hit near his home.

News media outlets from all over the world began picking up on Suter's unwanted air travel story after it appeared on the website of Springfield's daily *News-Leader*. Suter told of his adventure on Good Morning America, while declining an appearance on the Today Show. Suter's amazing tornado story also attracted the attention of comedians. Perhaps that's because the *News-Leader* reported how he was only wearing his boxer shorts when the tornado launched him into a field. That bit of information inspired news briefs all over the United States.

Weather writers marvel at items that tornadoes pick up and transplant hundreds of feet—or even miles away. Hollywood's movie epic *Twister* made much of flying cows. In the horrific "nader" that hit the Ozarks region in March 2006, that was no airborne bovine flying by in the storm—that was Matt Suter in his skivvies.

More than six hundred families were forced out of their demolished homes in the Caruthersville area after an evening tornado went on a rampage.

Storm Strength

F3

Number of Fatalities

2

Time and Location

6:10 PM on April 2, 2006; Braggadocio and Caruthersville

Braggadocio and Caruthersville are Pemiscot County communities that encountered the full force of nature's wrath on the Sunday evening of April 2, 2006. On God's appointed day of rest, the Devil did his worst work in Missouri's Bootheel area with an early season outbreak of tornadoes. Perhaps it's no surprise that the evil winds wreaked the most havoc on the houses of the holy in Caruthersville, a churchgoing town of about two thousand families.

Among the churches damaged or destroyed were Faith Missionary Baptist, Jesus Name Tabernacle, and St. John's Episcopal. More churches suffered disrespect and loss across the Mississippi River from Caruthersville in the states of Illinois and Tennessee.

Another significant casualty of the 2006 storm was the great landmark Caruthersville Cotton Warehouse. Once a giant swamp and dense forest of tall oaks, the Bootheel area was logged out and drained for farmland in the nineteenth century. King Cotton became its crop.

Caruthersville rests on the edge of that farmland, deep in the Bootheel, on the banks of the Mississippi. The old town has had at least five courthouses as the seat of Pemiscot County. Pemiscot is derived from a Native American word approximating "liquid mud." Indeed, the flatlands around Caruthersville often sink below the raging Mississippi in the river's perennial spring and summer floods.

Of course, the ultimate mayhem predicted for the county capital known as Caruthersville involves the nearby New Madrid Fault. When this fault finally erupts in the earthquake of the eons—the "big one" that will shake the U.S. continent—towns like Caruthersville are expected to sink and disappear below the liquid mud.

In the famous New Madrid Earthquake of 1811–1812, the mighty Mississippi shifted east to claim some of Illinois for the state of Missouri. Legends maintain that the great river ran backwards for a time. Fantastic geysers of mud, sand, and carbonized wood shot skyward from the lowlands and wetlands of Pemiscot County. However, on the evening of April 2, 2006, it's what came down from a darkened sky in a funnel of fury that terrorized the citizens of Caruthersville. More than six hundred families were forced out of what was left of their homes. The schools were gone, and the south side of the city was flattened.

On Monday morning, April 3, police barred entrance to the once-proud county seat. A group of disaster volunteers and American Red Cross emergency workers were allowed to enter the ailing town to start to pick up the pieces of lives shattered.

Damage and debris from the 2006 destruction has since vanished from Caruthersville, but many questions remain. What will nature serve up next for the proud seat of Pemiscot? Phenomenal flooding? Terrible earth tremors? Or more funnels of fury?

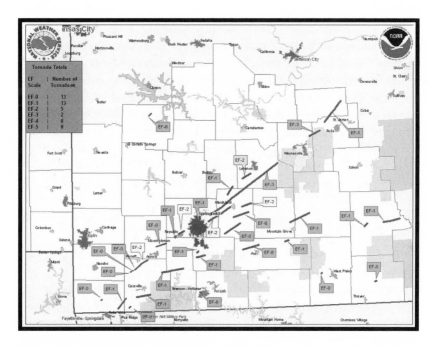

Tornado outbreaks put twisters on the ground traveling paths from southwest to northeast.

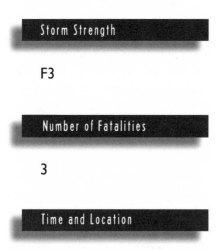

Storm Strength

F3

Number of Fatalities

3

Time and Location

6:25 PM on January 7, 2008; Springfield and Webster County

2008: Weather Fanatic's Day of Frenzy

Meteorologists tend to be obsessed with the weather from an early age, and that was certainly the case with Dave Snider when he was a youngster. He now handles the chaotic TV weather duties for station KYTV, the NBC affiliate in Springfield. A self-described "weather fanatic" who studied meteorology at Saint Louis University, Snider also is a weather photographer. Snider will sometimes shoot what he covers. When waves of tornadoes hit his viewership area on January 7, 2008, however, he was far too absorbed with his weather radar and warnings to worry about shooting any photographs outdoors.

Supercell thunderstorms were popping up all day—over and over again—along the same general area of I-44, explained Snider. In a twelve-hour period, there were 62 tornado warnings and 161 severe weather reports. Twisters were hitting trailer courts, picking up cars, knocking out power, and killing people along the I-44 corridor from the Missouri border to Marshfield.

"This event was unique in that it was the first time I felt that the news staff was in danger of being in the way of a tornado during our live coverage," said Snider of his KYTV colleagues. "At one point, I alerted our news staff it was time to move to the interior rooms.

"Thankfully, that particular storm bypassed the station," added Snider. "It did damage nearby. For about 10 minutes, I was afraid of the weather . . . and the studio lights and the tons of pea gravel on the rubber roof over my head in the studio."

Not everybody was receiving the tornado warnings and weather alerts sent out by TV stations. The storms came in a series—they "trained"—and some of the early turbulence knocked out electricity. Lights flickered, then were extinguished. Televisions went silent. Springfield and Joplin utilities reported thousands without power.

Between the storms, Rod Stelford of Republic looked over his smashed home and damaged business. The *Springfield News-Leader* reported that he advised his insurance agent on rebuilding. Pointing toward his house at 637 E. Wilson Street, he said: "Build back on that foundation—I want that basement."

Folks without basements sought refuge where they could. In tiny Strafford, one hundred people showed up at a shelter after a pair of twisters hit the community of about one thousand residents. Back-to-back storms frayed nerves and undid lives. To cap it all off, a squall line came through with record rainfall for the grand finale.

"It's not uncommon to see tornado outbreaks with numbers such as these," said Snider. "But to see such an event confined to one region—not to mention one TV market—is rare, if not unheard of. . . . Moreover, it was January and not the typical peak storm season. It left our viewership asking: What's going on with our weather?"

Weather radars lit up with tornadic activity on the deadly evening in May 2008 in the border area of Missouri and Oklahoma.

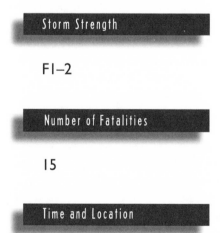

Storm Strength

FI–2

Number of Fatalities

15

Time and Location

5:59 PM on May 10, 2008; Seneca and Newton County

2008: Cars as Death Traps in Twisters

Expensive funeral caskets can look like late model cars. Sometimes cars of any year can become caskets, when marauding tornadoes seem to take aim at vehicles caught in the open during a violent storm. This is the kind of storm attack that happened on the second weekend in May 2008. High-top thunderheads began climbing to the ceiling of the sky in Kansas and in Oklahoma. Weather radars began showing ringed echoes and classic tornado signatures.

What hit the ground in Picher, Oklahoma, was no mere echo. It was big and brown and noisy. The twister picked up sheet metal, bank records, and home insulation and blew it all several counties away to the Missouri border and beyond. Six people died in Picher in a maelstrom of uprooted trees, crushed homes, and overturned cars.

The deadly storm rumbled east into Missouri and knocked the wind in and out of Seneca, a border town just south of I-44. Bodies were later discovered in a stretch of farm fields between the interstate and Seneca. Among the dead were five family members who had been on their way to a wedding when the tornado caught up with their vehicle. Susan Roberts told the Associated Press about a woman who tried to escape nature's wrath in a classic 1985 Cadillac. The vintage Cadillac ended up inside Roberts's destroyed living room. The desperate woman, who thought she had found a place to get away from the storm's terrifying violence, instead perished when the Cadillac became a death trap.

Television weathercasters like Lisa Teachman of KMBC-TV in Kansas City had the grim task of reporting the car deaths. She noted that the ten people who died in Missouri during the storm were killed "mainly as a result of taking shelter in their cars."

Cheryl Cobb of Missouri's Highway Patrol followed up with a statement to the news media about tornado safety for motorists. The press release noted that driving at high speed from a twister's path may only be a safe option if it is some distance away.

"If the tornado is bearing down on you, stop your vehicle off the traveled portion of the roadway and seek a sturdy shelter or lie flat in a ditch or low spot," noted Cobb. "If you are outside, remember to cover your head with your arms, coat, or blanket. Stopping on a roadway increases the chance of being struck by other motorists. Stopping under an overpass can cause a dangerous wind tunnel effect. Motorists may be struck by debris or blown out from under the bridge."

Get out of your vehicle and into a ditch or low spot? Easier said than done! What if you are traveling in the dark of night, punctuated only by streaks of lightning? What if all low areas are likely to be under water? What if you think you are driving into shafts of rain, rather than a twister?

Tornadoes generate the fastest winds on earth, which is why you are advised to get out of your car or mobile home and to seek protection elsewhere when a tornado has touched down near you.

Storm Strength

F1–2

Number of Fatalities

3

Time and Location

10:10 PM on May 13, 2009; Kirksville

2009: May Tornadoes in Kirksville

W hat a difference a century makes. Kirksville's killer tornado of 1899 brought terror and turmoil to the city. Rescue teams from nearby towns took hours to arrive. Piecing together what happened took days. News of the storm was detailed with ink on paper.

News of Kirksville's killer tornado of 2009 was a different story entirely. The tale was told electronically and with immediacy. Cable TV's Weather Channel gave audiences a look at the Kirksville twister along with updated forecasts on where the storm was tracking next in Missouri. Bloggers streamed videos of the storm taken with cell phones. TV stations from across Missouri sent teams for on-the-spot coverage. Kansas City TV offered viewers photo images of damage, video of the spinning twister, and updated stories. Website coverage was 24-7 by both newspapers and television stations in the state.

A summary of all the meteorological phenomena of the evening of May 13, 2009, was provided by the National Weather Service. According to the report, the Kirksville area saw three separate tornadoes touch down.

The first tornado appeared west of Kirksville and destroyed a mobile home. A woman was killed in that encounter. The second tornado formed to the west near Novinger and damaged power lines and several homes.

The third tornado went through northern Kirksville and was the most destructive. That tornado "exploded" a home and killed the couple living there. They were thrown about twenty-five yards from the site of the home. The tornado also destroyed or damaged dozens of homes, buildings, and a car dealership in the Kirksville area.

"Yes, my hometown got hit by a tornado tonight," wrote one blogger. "We get tornado reports every year, but they usually end up being nothing, but as I stepped outside the rain had stopped and so had the wind. The air was completely still. For those of us who live near tornadoes, you know this means you have one coming."

In a story on Kansas City's KMBC-TV website, station meteorologist Lisa Teachman told of an "elderly" mother and son whose car was pulled to the side of the road as the tornado grew closer. It blew out all of the windows in the car before it moved on to other destruction. On KMBC's comment post, readers debated what is meant by "elderly." Should the woman killed by the first tornado be called elderly in a story if she was just in her fifties?

Others posted complaints about TV programs being interrupted for the weather updates and tornado reports. They were countered by those who argued that the reports are necessary and do save lives in severe weather. In Kirksville's tornado of 1899, no one cut into TV programs with special bulletins. There were no televisions, no videos, no bloggers. There were no cameras for memorial services for the forty-five citizens lost in the 1899 tornado.

II. Lightning and Hail

en Franklin would be proud. Our knowledge about lightning has come a long way since old Ben rigged up his famous kite experiment in 1752. We now know that lightning can travel as fast as sixty thousand miles per second and generate temperatures much hotter than the sun.

Franklin might be even more amazed to learn that we have discovered new kinds of lightning in recent decades. We now know about "elves," short flashes of electricity that blaze high above the clouds near the edge of outer space. We also now know about "sprites," which can come in many shapes and several different colors. Then there are "jets," conical blasts of electrical light that last for under one second, high above the thunderclouds. Elves, sprites, and jets are all fantastic phenomena that occur high above the storm clouds in the stratosphere and beyond. However, for the purposes of this book, the more mundane "cloud-to-ground" lightning provides quite enough to write about.

Missouri's Mark Twain knew nothing of elves and sprites, but he was plenty impressed with the common variety of lightning. From an early age, it scared the devil out of him. As a youngster, Twain thought lightning and thunder contained messages from the Almighty—and they were not friendly love notes.

Later in life, Twain used the flash and clatter in the sky to illustrate literary points. "The difference between the almost right word and the right word is really a large matter—it's the difference between the lightning bug and the lightning."

When work commenced on this section of *Nature's Wrath* about the history of lightning in Missouri, I was concerned as to whether I would find enough words—never mind the right words—about lightning. My worries were put to rest after discovering how many lightning rod businesses are located in the state of Missouri. The difference between the words of PR lightning safety advisories and the lingo of those who climb high to install rods is "the difference between the lightning bug and the lightning," as Mark Twain might say. These rod installation experts are colorful characters, and they have enough storm anecdotes for a separate lightning weather book entirely.

Lightning rod experts told me about multi-volt bolts out of the blue hitting scout camps, golfers, firemen, as well as clock towers, billboards, and church spires. They also told me about installing rods to capture lightning on barns and silos, nuclear power plant towers, and the scoreboard at Kauffman Stadium in Kansas City.

One of my favorite sources turned out to be none other than J. Seamus Donohue, a.k.a. "Lightning Rod Man." Donohue insisted that he harbors no religious bias, but he said it's his experience that God is much more likely to damage a Protestant church with a lightning hit than a Catholic church.

According to Donohue, with a Catholic church, the head priest usually makes the decision for a rod system and pays to have the job done right. With Protestant churches, a committee makes the decision for a rod system and compromises to save money with an inferior installation. The results can be catastrophic.

* * * * *

Hail: A Horrible Plague

Both lightning and hail get some prominent mention in the Bible. Hail happened to be one of several horrible plagues to befall Egypt in the time of Moses. However, it's not necessary to go back to Old Testament times to experience hail at its worst. According to the Missouri Climate Center, the residents of this state encounter a thunderstorm with hail about three times per year. Most of the time, hail in Missouri is of the pea-sized variety, although hail the size of softballs has accompanied severe thunderstorms throughout the state's weather history.

Missouri cannot claim the largest hailstone in the history of the world. However, the neighboring state of Nebraska does have that distinction. The Missouri Climate Center reports that a 7-inch-diameter hailstone with a circumference of 18.75 inches fell in Aurora, Nebraska, on June 22, 2003.

The Cornhuskers may be able to claim the largest hailstone ever, but Tiger Town in Missouri can lay claim to one of the deepest pile-ups of hail in American history. Columbia experienced a covering of hail about three feet deep in 1911. In recent years, hail has covered southwest portions of Missouri with an icy carpet several inches thick, but nothing approaches the freak 1911 storm.

Missouri was in the crosshairs of the costliest hailstorm in U.S. history. The I-70 corridor hailstorm of April 10, 2001, caused more than $2 billion in damage with most of the destruction in the north St. Louis area. Florissant mayor Robert Lowery remembers the hailstorm as a noisy nightmare that took years to recover from. Very few homes in his city were without severe hail damage from the storm that brought tornadoes to other parts of the state. "My advice to anybody who finds themselves outside in a storm like that is to seek shelter immediately," said Lowery. "You can't wait to see if it will stop, or if it gets worse. When you are at Ground Zero in the Storm of the Century, it's time to take cover."

Missouri's Mark Twain had important things to say about lightning bugs and lightning.

Typically, bolts of lightning travel at speeds that can reach 60,000 miles per second.

Summer of 1842; Hannibal

1842: Lightning Scars Hannibal Boy

Most accounts in this collection of weather mayhem can be considered reasonably factual—and occasionally even beyond reproach. This particular piece, however, is based on hearsay evidence, unproveable conjecture, and expired literary license.

This much is true: A young boy named Samuel Clemens, growing up in the 1840s in Hannibal, Missouri, was profoundly affected by thunderstorms which shattered his sleep and peace of mind. Later, as writer Mark Twain, he recalled how he hated the late-night thunder and lightning. Twain remembered the fright he felt from the clash and clamor of storms in the dark. He was convinced they were sent as a visible reminder of his lapses from a vengeful God. They were sent to inform him that all of his earlier misdeeds had not gone unnoticed.

It's a reasonable conjecture that some of the storms, which terrorized the young boy, occurred in the late spring and summer of 1842 when he was six. That was a time of torment for the young Sam Clemens, as he lost his brother, Benjamin, who died at age nine of a bilious fever.

The six-year-old Clemens was forced by his mother to put his hand on the face of the corpse in a bid of farewell. The experience gave him nightmares. He felt a burden of guilt, as though he was somehow responsible for an evil that took his brother's breath away.

Is it unreasonable to suggest that the summer storms of that year of 1842 were especially hard on the boy's nerves? What must young Sammy have thought, quaking alone in his bed, when bolts of lightning thrashed about and the night skies opened in the summer darkness of 1842? This much we do know: When Twain was moved to offer his gems of wisdom, they sometimes reflected the impact of lightning and thunder on his life. His wise musings on nature's noisiest acts of insolence were many.

Here is a Twain observation: "The fear of lightning is one of the most distressing infirmities a human being can be afflicted with."

Here is another oft-quoted Twain observation: "Thunder is good, thunder is impressive, but it is lightning that does all the work."

Twain knew what the scientists now know. The bang and rumble of thunder is simply a storm's growling. It is so much hot air that was once cold—until the lightning got hold of it. Lightning is the bite. Thunder is the bark. It's lightning that causes the noisy shock wave, which signals the sky's anger.

Here is Twain's comment to the New England Society on thunder: "When the thunder commences to merely tune up, and scrape up, and saw, and key up the instruments for the performance, strangers say: 'Why, what awful thunder you have here!' But when the baton is raised and the real concert begins, you'll find that stranger down in the cellar, with his head in the ash barrel."

Legislators aren't the only ones making noise in Jefferson City. In 1911, a loud thunder signaled a bolt of lightning that set the capitol ablaze.

A bolt can heat the air in its path up to 50,000 degrees Fahrenheit.

February 11, 1911; Jefferson City

1911: BLUE BOLT SETS CAPITOL ABLAZE

State capitols are awe-inspiring affairs: stately churches of democracy. Solid architectural features typically adorn these places for conducting the people's business—and that business is often performed under a towering dome of grand proportion. However, these great domes are made by man. There is no guarantee that they will withstand the forces of nature. In the case of lightning, those forces can be measured in electrical megawatts per meter, which generate temperatures several times higher than those found on the sun's surface.

An average bolt of blue lightning carries an electrical current in the range of forty thousand amperes and creates a supersonic shock wave. However, the streak of lightning that hit the dome of the statehouse in Jefferson City, Missouri, on February 11, 1911, wasn't your average bolt of blue.

The bolt reportedly emerged from a dark storm cloud rumbling in from the west—a rolling cloud "seething with lightning" and ready to produce consternation and anarchy in the very seat of Missouri's government. When the bolt hit, it started a fire that was beyond the capabilities of the horse-drawn fire wagons and primitive firefighting equipment housed in several wards throughout Jefferson City.

Bob Priddy, a veteran of the capitol press corps, has spent countless hours researching statehouse history in Jefferson City. According to Priddy, there were several witnesses to the lightning that destroyed the capitol. "A four-year-old boy, visiting his grandmother's house about six blocks south of the capitol, just happened to look out her kitchen window to see a massive bolt of lightning streak across the sky," writes Priddy. "The ensuing blast of thunder made him believe he had seen a comet, and the thunder made him think the comet had exploded."

Closer to the capitol, the governor was entertaining state officials and reporters at the Governor's Mansion. His wife was upstairs writing a letter when the bolt struck. She was certain it had hit the mansion. Smoke and flames from the capitol roof area made it clear where the lightning hit. The governor and reporters dashed into the building to save documents and files. They were unable to save gigantic paintings in the House and Senate chambers by Missouri's great artist George Caleb Bingham. They were forced to retreat from the fire.

According to Priddy, one witness said the copper cladding of the dome glowed cherry red from heat before collapsing. Another said Old Glory flew from its pole throughout most of the fire until, at last, the flames ate through its ropes. This American flag was last seen burning, floating north out over the wide Missouri River.

Not everyone regretted the loss of the old capitol. A much larger building replaced it with a dome rising 238 feet above ground level.

Big Oak Tree State Park, south of East Prairie, is a refuge for tall oaks and other trees that once covered the Missouri Bootheel. Many of its champion oaks have been lost to lightning strikes.

Factoid

Though Missouri seems to have its fair share of lightning strikes, Florida is actually the lightning capital of the U.S.

Time and Location

May 5, 1905; Big Oak Tree State Park

1952: R.I.P. Champ Show Me Tree

A dense forest of tall, old-growth hardwoods once blanketed an area of Missouri now often referred to as Swampeast. In this bootheel region of the state, many towering oaks and elms once reached into the heavens and tempted the lightning to strike from storms rolling across the Mississippi River Valley.

Lightning did, in fact, oblige and wreaked a bit of wrath and vengeance on the tall trees. However, the deadly bolts could never decimate, or even dent, such a vast stand of timber. Leave it to the logging companies to finally do the decimating of deciduous growth in the Missouri Bootheel. Logging companies began tearing away at the thick tree forests early in the 1880s. By the Great Depression era of the 1930s, literally hundreds of thousands of acres of trees were felled. The flatlands left behind were drained for crop use.

Residents of Mississippi County were motivated to save the little forest heritage remaining in the 1930s, after they learned of some rare champion trees left standing. Among those trees was a 143-foot-tall champion oak—its trunk more than 20 feet wide—with more than three centuries of growing history under its bark. The successful campaign to save the last piece of giant forest enlisted schoolchildren who collected pennies; businesses that provided dollars; and small-town and big-city newspapers supporting the cause with ink. A segment of forest was saved and became Big Oak Tree State Park.

Sadly, the great tree of trees in the park was lost. Twice it was hit and scarred by lightning bolts, and in 1952, the revered Bur Oak succumbed. A cross section of the stately tree now is displayed in a casket of glass at Big Oak Tree State Park.

Lightning can be traumatic for trees and those who care for them. A 334-year-old tree such as Missouri's revered Bur Oak cannot be replaced. Interestingly enough, some of the oldest trees in America are actually being wired now with lightning protection to save them from the Bur Oak's fate.

"We're rodding a lot of trees now," said Preferred Lightning Protection's Ken Pettlon of Maryville, Missouri. "We're doing champion trees in the New Madrid area and landscape trees at Lake of the Ozarks. We have even wired a tree at the home of Harry S. Truman in Independence."

Pettlon said homeowners believe that trees around their residences will attract lightning and deflect it from hitting their homes. Not so, he said. "We had a fellow in an underground home in Buffalo who thought a stand of trees above his home kept him safe," said Pettlon. "The lightning hit his trees, traveled down, then jumped into his house. It traveled along the pipes in his house, blew up his toilet, then exploded the methane in his septic tank. He called and had us rod his trees for protection after that."

Lightning strikes in the great outdoors have caused trauma on Scouting trips, including a campout at Taum Sauk Mountain State Park.

Factoid

On average, lightning causes ninety-three casualties in the United States every year.

Time and Location

July 2000; Taum Sauk Mountain State Park

2000: BOY SCOUT LIGHTNING STRIKE

"**W**hen thunder roars, go indoors." That's been the slogan for lightning safety awareness campaigns across the country for years. Unfortunately, "indoors" often is not an easy option for Boy Scouts on camping trips in tents in the great outdoors.

It's not hard to find tragic tales of Scouts caught in the worst that nature has to offer—whether it's tornadic winds, pelting rain and hail, or lightning bolts out of the blue. In July of 2000, four Missouri Scouts suffered injuries when their tent at Taum Sauk Mountain State Park was struck near the town of Ironton.

Scout leaders generally get high marks for taking care of their young charges in both urban settings and on those extended expeditions into the wilderness. However, one dramatic blemish on their record concerns the number of lightning casualties over recent years of outdoor activities.

Between 1995 and 2006, a study of newspaper archives and Associated Press stories showed that seven Scouts and Scout leaders have been killed and fifty injured in fifteen incidents involving camping or outdoor events. Those statistics were cited in a *Los Angeles Times* account of the death of a sixteen-year-old Scout during a one-week camping trip at the Resica Falls Scout Reservation in the Pocono Mountains of Pennsylvania. Experts on lightning said the death of the teen Scout in 2002, which occurred after a rogue bolt hit his campsite tent pole, was preventable. They also termed the Boy Scouts' record on lightning safety in America as questionable.

Arizona lightning expert David Holle wrote a court brief in the 2002 fatality and stated that "If only on the basis of hearing thunder and seeing the flashes during the day, trained people should have kept everyone [indoors] in the dining hall."

Leaders with the Greater St. Louis Area Council for the Boy Scouts of America insist that a new program for weather safety has been put in place since the 2000 Taum Sauk incident in Missouri and the 2002 fatal lightning event in Pennsylvania. The Scouts' severe weather training program can be located online at www.scouting.org. The site includes a "Guide to Safe Camping" tailored for Scouts and Scout leaders with a section devoted to lightning safety.

Boy Scouts of America send about 1 million boys into the outdoors every summer. Lightning-safety advocates argue that training in the dangers posed by weather events should be mandatory for Scout leaders. At the least, they argue:

• A detailed lightning safety plan should be in place for camps and any outdoor activities. All trips should be preceded by weather monitoring.

• Leaders should abide by the "30-Minute Rule" that restricts activities to the indoors for one-half hour after the last visible lightning bolt is observed. Tents do not count as "indoors."

Lightning can be beautiful and awe-inspiring, but it also can be deadly, as a funeral party near Willard found out in August 2002.

Most human lightning strikes occur in June, July, and August.

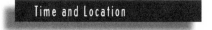

August 23, 2002; Willard

2002: Flaming Bolt Jolts a Funeral

One of the most bizarre—and most deadly—lightning blasts ever to mar the lives of Missourians occurred in a rural cemetery not far from the town of Springfield on Friday, August 23, 2002. It seems that everyone in the business of lightning protection in Missouri knows this horrible tale.

"I know lots of bad stories about lightning," said J. Seamus Donohue, who refers to himself as the "Lightning Rod Man". "There's the terrible story of the kids killed by lightning in Swope Park in Kansas City, but by far the weirdest hit has to be about the fatal lightning strike at a morning funeral down near Springfield."

The tragedy happened during graveside services at a funeral at the Clear Creek Cemetery just west of Willard. About thirty-five people were in attendance to say their final farewells to eighty-three-year-old Leon Carroll. Witnesses said it was sprinkling outside when suddenly a bolt came from out of nowhere and sent a ball of fire down a tree near the grave. Those standing under the tree were bowled over. Two died immediately, and two more died from subsequent injuries after being rushed to a Springfield hospital.

"The best buddies of this man show up to say goodbye, and they end up getting killed at his funeral. It's just pretty weird," said the Lightning Rod Man, who owns Donohue's Lightning Protection. "They went through the war together, but then lightning takes them out years later. My theory is Mr. Carroll did not want to go up and face St. Peter alone, he sort of wanted his buddies along with him. Any time you stand under a tree during a storm you are asking for it," said Donohue. "But they weren't in the middle of a violent storm. It was barely a shower at that cemetery."

Fire Chief Gary Wirth with the Willard Fire Protection District was one of the first on the scene at the Clear Creek Cemetery disaster. He said the people at the graveside were dazed, confused, and still had their umbrellas out in the rain.

"There was a pastor there giving CPR to some of the downed folks when we arrived," recalled Wirth. "We found remnants of the umbrellas from those hit. The plastic handles were melted and the nylon umbrella tops were completely disintegrated."

"That sight still gives me pause," said Wirth. "I keep my eyes on the horizon now to see if there is any lightning in the distance, because you don't have to be right in the middle of a storm to get hit by lightning. That was the first and only fatal lightning event I dealt with in my thirty years of fire service. That sight at the cemetery made an impression on me."

After the stricken were evacuated from the cemetery, all the remaining mourners joined in prayer on behalf of their fellow mourners hit by lightning. The funeral in Willard has to go down as one of the strangest ever.

Lightning naturally gravitates to the highest structures in the area of storms, and that can mean clock towers, church spires, and weathervanes are vulnerable.

Every year, lightning is the source of hundreds of millions of dollars in damage to forestry and property.

August 1, 2003; Frontenac

2003: Frontenac Clock Tower Hit

For centuries, clock towers have given people reliable time through both eye and ear. Moving dials have provided the visual component for these elevated timepieces, and often clock chimes have provided a familiar audio indication of time. On August 1, 2003, time seemed to stop at the clock tower at the Hilton Hotel in the swank St. Louis suburb of Frontenac. Waves of thunderstorms were training through the metro area that early morning, and a few were accompanied by fierce lightning.

Just as the clock in the Hilton's hotel tower was about to strike 6 a.m., a bolt of lightning hit the hotel roof in the vicinity of the clock tower itself. The instantaneous crash of thunder provided an audio wakeup call for the hotel guests, many asleep in the upper-floor rooms.

Guests were evacuated from the hotel, as anxious firefighters arrived to address the smoldering clock tower from a fire that resulted from the strike. Several alarms were sounded, and firefighters arrived in the rain from Frontenac and other nearby suburban cities.

Clock towers are a natural for lightning strikes, according to David Robbins of Maryville, Missouri. His Robbins Lightning Protection Inc. began rodding barns and grain silos in the early 1900s and by the late twentieth century was installing lightning safety devices on the cooling towers at nuclear power plants.

"Lightning naturally gravitates to the highest structures in the area of a storm and that can mean clock towers are most at risk," said Robbins. "With some hits, the lightning will seem to explode into fire like a stick of dynamite. Other times, it will hit, and it will take a while for a full-blown fire to appear," Robbins added.

Some clock towers are fabricated with decorative weather vanes that also act as lightning rods. In a very intense storm, the air surrounding the metallic rod becomes ionized and highly conductive. When lightning hits, the ideal outcome is that the electricity is safely conveyed from rod to earth through a grounded cable.

The hit on the hotel in Frontenac made headlines in the St. Louis news, but by far the most famous clock tower lightning strike was at the fictional Clock Tower in Hill Valley, California. That strike hit in 1955 and stopped the clock cold in a popular movie called *Back to the Future*, starring Michael J. Fox. In the Fox movie, the old eccentric scientist, Emmett "Doc" Brown, tries to harness the electricity from the lightning for his back-to-the-future mobile. The lightning strike was the most dramatic scene in the movie.

"Our clock tower is in a small little steeple at the back of the hotel," said Al Sedlacek at the Frontenac Hilton. "The lightning strike caused a lot of commotion, but the clock was ticking after the hit and continues to tick."

Multiple cloud-to-ground lightning strikes emphasize the necessity to get indoors when thunderstorms are in the vicinity.

Despite the common misconception, rubber sole shoes and tires actually provide very little protection from lightning strikes.

July 16, 2004; Lee's Summit

2004: LEE'S SUMMIT CHIEF STRIKE

Scientists tell us that lightning is not distributed evenly around the planet. Areas near oceans often are more prone to lightning strikes than regions farther inland. In America, Florida gets tagged by many more heavenly discharges than the state of Missouri. In the wee hours of July 16, 2004, however, Kansas Citians would have argued they were getting more than their fair share of lightning bolts.

Intense lightning set off several fires in populated areas of Jackson County. In the Kansas City suburbs, firefighters were called out to douse a number of blazes with origins traced to early morning thunderstorms. Fire Battalion Chief Jim Eden watched the angry storms roll into his town of Lee's Summit, east of Kansas City, from an interstate overpass on I-470. Eden was on weather spotting duty in order to provide advanced warning of any severe turbulence heading toward the area.

"It was about 3:30 in the morning, and the storm sirens were going off," recalled Eden. "I just got on my phone to make a report inside my car when suddenly a huge ball of light flashed inside and around my car. All the lights on my dash lit up, and then the car was filled with smoke."

The dash lights no sooner went dead when Eden's car began to be showered with gravel and pieces of pavement ripped from the interstate. Although Eden was disoriented, he still managed to jump out the door to find his car roof glowing a hot red. Antennae on the car were no longer extended, but reduced to silver blobs.

"I was definitely in shock," said Eden. "It was like I was in a Faraday Chamber, the electricity surrounded me, but fortunately it did not go through me. The rivets in the car doors and chassis actually melted."

Eden had experienced something dangerous and unique. He has since studied the phenomenon of lightning and has a new respect for it. He has no interest in becoming another Roy Cleveland Sullivan, a Virginia park ranger who was hit by lightning seven times before his death in 1983. In one strike, Sullivan was blasted out of his car, and his hair set afire. In another, he was knocked unconscious. His fellow Shenandoah National Park rangers nicknamed him the Human Lightning Conductor.

After his own encounter, Fire Chief Eden earned the dubious nickname of Sparky. He said his colleagues also joked that it was taking a big risk to volunteer to go weather spotting with Sparky. Eden said that, months later, after it sank in that he was hit by lightning, he found less humor in his brush with a lightning bolt.

"I've been on several lightning strikes on paramedic duty. The outcomes are not always so good for those involved," said Chief Eden. "I am a lot more cautious about being outside when storms are in the vicinity."

Although scores of people in the United States survive lightning hits every year, they often are plagued by permanent nervous system disorders.

Golfers' cleated shoes can make them especially good lightning rods and electric conductors.

May 7, 2007; St. Charles

2007: St. Paul Repeat in St. Charles

"I have seen the Lord, he has appeared to me, he has manifested himself also to me," declared Saul of Taurus after being hit by a blinding bolt of light on the Road to Damascus. The stricken Saul was later canonized as a saint—St. Paul. Two thousand years later, two more of the Lord's ministers by the names of Kevin Hughes and Don Erehart also encountered a great bolt. They were on their way to a green at Whitmoor Country Club in St. Charles.

The two young pastors at First Evangelical Church in Manchester, Missouri, were not aware a storm was in the vicinity of their golf game. They did see lightning in the skies in the distance, but they were not worried. Suddenly, a bolt from above sent a tremendous surge of electrical energy through their bodies. Hughes and Erehart both smelled an acrid burning, just after the lightning seemed to exit through their golf shoes. As with the stricken Saul, the lightning gave the two travelers on the links in St. Charles a lot to think about. It made them firm believers in the incalculable power from above.

"Don and I were getting ready to tee off, when this explosion out of nowhere went off right where we were standing," said Hughes. "It was out of the blue—totally unexpected."

"A huge charge came through the top of my head and out my foot. I felt it very clearly," added Hughes. "There was a silver dollar–sized patch that tingled on the top of my head for about six months. I also had quite a headache for about six months."

Hughes said he has friends who continue to golf even when there's a threat of lightning. They expose themselves to danger in the face of National Weather Service statistics that show about seventy-five deaths and many more serious injuries from lightning occur every year in the United States. "I have a friend in Colorado who is a golfing fanatic and has been hit three times," said Hughes. "He keeps golfing in lightning even after serious damage to his nervous system. I've changed my ways. If it looks like it's stormy outside, I get myself inside."

Like Saul of Taurus, the Reverend Hughes has seen the light. Of course, it can be argued that Saul, later St. Paul, had a conversion of more consequence. He became a minister of sorts himself and began instilling religious belief instead of persecuting those with religious convictions.

Only recently have some in the medical community suggested that St. Paul may have been hit by lightning on that Road to Damascus. He experienced an explosion of light resulting in temporary loss of sight, disorientation, and other symptoms consistent with a lightning injury. Reverend Hughes prefers not speculate on the lightning strike theory about St. Paul. He said he is just glad he and St. Paul both lived to tell about their enlightening experience.

At 630 feet tall, the St. Louis Gateway Arch is grounded directly into bedrock and is able to withstand hundreds of lightning strikes each year.

The average lightning bolt is six miles long.

August 16, 2007; St. Louis

2007: St. Louis Church Spire Strike

At night, the towering spire of the church known as the "Rock" on North Grand Boulevard in St. Louis is a bright beacon and a jewel of reflected light. The church and its spire are an anchor for Midtown and the revitalized Grand Center neighborhood.

All was nearly lost on a wickedly stormy August evening in 2007 when lightning struck the 135-year-old church spire and nearly destroyed a much-loved monument to faith. The Rock, otherwise known as the St. Alphonsus Liguori Catholic Church, got its nickname from the sturdy exterior limestone walls of the church and a rock wall bordering the property.

Church towers always have been vulnerable to lightning strikes, and the Rock was no exception. Early on, Christian churches in old Europe attempted to discourage lightning hits through prayers by the clergy. One prayer by Catholic priests asked that the Almighty temper the destruction of hail and cyclones and the force of tempests and lightning. Prayers were not as effective as the lightning rod invention discovered by Benjamin Franklin in 1749.

Interestingly enough, some clergy resisted Franklin's invention and insisted the rods would attract more lightning. Other clergy argued that churches would be, in effect, trying to defy the will of God by placing rods on church roofs to ward off his lightning. Franklin had no patience for such arguments. By that kind of logic, Franklin argued, the churches should remove their roofs that thwart the rain that God wills upon the earth.

Reverend Matthew Bonk of the Rock Catholic Church in St. Louis said Franklin was up against Calvinist thought in Boston. He said there is no argument against lightning rods in the Catholic Church doctrine. "We definitely have lightning rods at St. Alphonsus now that the church has been repaired," said Bonk. "I am sure we had them when the spire was hit in 2007, though they had to be very old with a church of 140 years."

"The lightning hit the spire, and we had fire within forty-five minutes," recalled Bonk. "It was a tremendous hit, and crash, and the hair was raised on everybody around the church. I had just arrived from Chicago, and here the church was burning down in front of me. Everybody was in shock."

Firefighters performed valiantly to save the church. The sanctuary and the inside of the Rock were destroyed, but the walls and the stained glass windows were largely intact. Twenty months of repair work costing about $12 million brought the Rock back as the blessed rock of salvation.

"It was a tragedy, but it could have been so much worse," said Bonk. "We could have lost the whole church and had casualties. The firefighters were so careful to save as much as they could. The people of our parish stayed together and struggled to bring the Rock back to its glory."

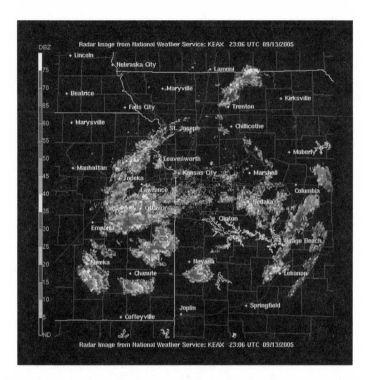

About 80 percent of lightning bolts in a thunderstorm stay within the cloud formations, but the 20 percent that hit the ground cause havoc.

Literally thousands of fires are started by lightning strikes in the U.S. each year.

July 22, 2008; Boone County

The carnival at the Boone County Fair in Columbia can be the highlight of the summer for kids in central Missouri. There's a giant Ferris wheel and thrill rides like the Super Slide, Cliff Hanger, High Roller, Dragon Wagon, and Tornado. In addition, there are competitions: pony pulls, tractor pulls, pedal pulls, draft horse pulls, pig races, ham judging, and the contest to see who will be named Miss Boone County. In the midst of all this, there's the auditory bliss of talent show singers, carousel music, and tunes by seasoned fiddlers.

All of this fun came to an abrupt halt on a warm evening in July 2008 when huge storm clouds coupled up in western Missouri and then trained through Boone County. Spider-vein flashes of lightning and crashes of thunder continued for hours, long after the fairgrounds were evacuated.

"I remember that evening because we got the word that high winds and lots of lightning were on their way," said Gale Blomenkamp, the chief of the Boone County Fire Protection District. "The Fair Board made the decision to shut down everything by 10 p.m. based on some advice from us. It was the wise thing to do, because activities don't wind down until well after midnight."

"People just don't understand why they are cleared out and things get shut down before the weather starts to even turn bad," said Blomenkamp. "We were worried about lightning strikes. It can strike as far away as ten miles from the storm front."

When the noisy storm front rolled through, it also began rolling up some nasty weather statistics, including lightning fires, medical emergencies, power outages, and accident calls. "The lightning caused so many power surges that we had alarms going off all over the place," said Gary L. Warren, battalion chief for the Columbia Fire Department. "We have to take every alarm seriously, and we respond as well as we can, but we get inundated in storms like the one that shut down the Boone County Fair."

More than four thousand homes were without power in Columbia because of the summer storm. Downed electrical transmission lines caused not only outages, but traffic problems as well.

However, the bigger problem was too much power as electrical surges from lightning fried the internal workings of all manner of appliances. Storm casualties included toasters, blenders, washing machines, freezers, microwaves, refrigerators, cordless phone bases, freezers, and, of course, televisions and computers. "Surge protection strips do work, but they're not 100 percent effective," said Chief Warren. "Often, the home circuit breakers don't work because the surge of electricity is coming the other way. The surge comes down to the breakers, instead of through them. The best way to save all your gadgets in a big storm is to unplug them."

Power surges from lightning hits destroy electrical distribution systems in homes every year, as well as countless electrical appliances.

Lightning can, in fact, strike the same place twice.

April 22, 2008; Kansas City

2008: LIGHTNING LIGHTS UP KANSAS CITY

Many Kansas City residents were rudely awakened on April 22, 2008, when a storm system lit up the early morning skies with varied, luminous electrical discharges—lightning.

In addition to the unusual amount of light flashing from the clouds, the storm complex was accompanied by what were described as excessive levels of acoustic echoing—thunder. However, most firefighters in the Kansas City area were concerned about the electrostatic discharges, not their companion audible shockwaves. The lightning was sparking fires from the Overland Park suburbs on the west to the hometown of Harry S. Truman, Independence, on the east.

"Lightning has done some pretty strange things in Kansas City," said Bud Van-Sickle, executive director of the Lightning Protection Institute in northwest Missouri. VanSickle once installed lightning rods and safety systems, before his work with the institute. Many of his jobs were in the Kansas City area, both before and after lightning hits.

"One of the weirdest home hits in Kansas City came through a picture window, traveled down the basement stairs to the electric box," recalled VanSickle. "It turned on the furnace and froze the thermostat, so it wouldn't shut off. It was 95 degrees out, so the homeowners were not happy."

In the case of the frozen furnace controls, VanSickle said the entire electrical wiring in the home had to be replaced. VanSickle remembered the story of another Kansas City home that was struck on the roof by lightning three times in one year. "Shingles were blown off each time, but there never was a fire," VanSickle explained. "This was a ranch home—not real high. It was in the middle of a row of homes—not on a hill. Why did it keep getting hit?"

"We were installing rods on the neighbors' homes, and we asked why the owners of the damaged home did not ask for an installation," recalled VanSickle. "The neighbors said the house was empty. The owners moved." Obviously, the victims of the multiple lightning hits chose a For Sale sign over a lightning rod or exorcist.

In Kansas City's April 22, 2008, lightning storm, fires started from strikes throughout the area. One hit that could have resulted in tragedy was at the American Inn on Interstate 70 near Independence. A driver on I-70 saw the lightning strike a neon sign atop the American Inn. The Good Samaritan pulled off the highway and alerted the front desk, then helped awaken guests to get them out of harm's way. The responding fire crews extinguished a small fire on the roof and, fortunately, no one suffered any injuries.

"Anything that sticks up in the air is a candidate for a strike, including American Inn signs," said VanSickle. "But, practically speaking, you just can't rod everything for lightning."

Ever since the invention of the automobile, car owners have had to worry about costly hail damage to their exteriors.

Hail Diameter

1.5–2.0 inches

Wind Gust

Unavailable

Time and Location

April 29, 1919; Columbia

1919: Plague of Hail in Columbia

One of the many horrible plagues to befall Egypt at the time of the prophet Moses involved a pounding hailstorm. The Old Testament God was not above using great punishing chunks of ice from the skies to smite wayward and wicked populations.

In the Book of Ezekiel, an angry Lord promised his people deliverance through the use of some of the most diabolical meteorological devices at his disposal. Enemies were destined to feel his wrath in an "overflowing shower in mine anger, and great hailstones in my fury."

The Israelites saw their enemies placed on the receiving end of divinely delivered hail on a number of occasions. After the famed biblical warrior Joshua surprised the Amorite Army in a successful night raid, the poor rascals got an extra dose of smiting from the heavens above. "And as they [Amorites] fled before Israel, while they were going down the ascent of Beth-horon, the Lord threw down great stones from heaven upon them as far as Azekah, and they died." There were more who died because of the hailstones than the men of Israel killed with the sword.

In 1919 A.D., a quite similar, if less lethal, hailstorm was visited upon the small college town of Columbia in mid-Missouri. Folks in Columbia had to wonder what offense they must have committed to be visited with such vengeful weather. Undoubtedly, some must have asked whether the storm was mistakenly sent their way, when it was likely intended for the politicians nearby in Jefferson City.

Hailstones in the 1911 Columbia storm ranged from golfball size to larger proportions. Weather experts today explain that stones of this size require huge, dark cumulonimbus clouds for their genesis. In these cloud towers over central Missouri, millions of frozen raindrops combine again and again, growing into something awful, yet awe-inspiring.

Three things stand out in all the accounts about the 1911 Columbia hailstorm: noise levels, depth of the stones on the ground, and the length of their presence. The clatter of the storm was said to be alarming, akin to thousands of toy false teeth wound up in an eerie, endless chatter. Add to this intense audio assault the disturbing sight of stones piling up to a depth of three feet—with even higher drifts of hail. Indeed, this was a plague that would have given any Egyptian pharaoh pause, much less the humble citizens of Columbia.

Finally, the stuff wouldn't leave. It totally covered all green vegetation. It trampled and smothered the colorful flowers of spring. It arrived on April 29, and on May 3, 1919, there were still icy remnants of the disaster.

A line of states just east of the Rocky Mountains is often referred to as Hail Alley. Nothing to hit the alley quite matches the Columbia event. Ezekiel would have been impressed.

Hail diameter depends on the number of round trips the stones make in the updrafts and downdrafts within storm clouds.

Hail Diameter

3 inches

Wind Gust

60 mph

Time and Location

April 3, 1974; St. Louis

1974: Green Skies, Hail in St. Louis

One of the most popular tenets in the vast category of weather folklore concerns green skies. When squally clouds turn ominously green, a widely held presumption is that they signal an impending onslaught of hail and tornadic winds.

On April 3, 1974, the skies west of the St. Louis area piled up with dark clouds. They formed a squall line that extended for hundreds of miles. By the time this unruly wall of wrath began to blast its way through the counties of eastern Missouri, national weather experts knew they were on the edge of a major meteorological event—one for the record books.

Folks on the ground knew that trouble was brewing because the wall of clouds was turning green. And St. Louis residents know enough about weather mayhem to read the signs in the heavens above. When a storm turns green, it's high time to take cover and run for the basement. The tall stack of clouds began to manufacture hailstones. Updrafts of wind pushed ice crystals into colder layers of air at the top of the cloud deck. Downdrafts carried the ice particles back to where moisture added more bulk. Then the roller coaster ride in the sky repeated itself many times—until the hailstones started falling to the earth. St. Louis was part of the stretch of land where the large hail pummeled homes, broke windows, dimpled cars, and dented siding. Some of the hail balls measured close to three inches in diameter. They were carried sideways by gusts clocked at sixty miles per hour.

The green clouds brought torrential rains, large hail, and damaging winds, as the weathermen say. Some funnel clouds were reported, but tornadoes did not find their way to the ground from those green skies until the supercells blew into Illinois, Indiana, Kentucky, and Ohio.

Out of St. Louis, the storm earned distinction as the "Super Tornado Outbreak of 1974". The worst carnage from the April twister attack occurred in Xenia, Ohio. Ohio lost more than thirty-five people with thirteen hundred injured in the storm. Survivors recalled the sky's "green tint" before catastrophe hit.

A quarter century after the great St. Louis hailstorm and the tornado outbreak, *Scientific American* printed an article meant to debunk the green skies mythology of severe storms. The scientists declared that neither hail nor tornado formation have any proven connection with green skies. If the sky turns green during a thunderstorm, there is scant evidence to support the theory that tornadoes or hail are about to be unleashed, the scientists insisted. They did remark that after fifteen years of scientific observation, there was some evidence for the existence of green thunderstorms.

Science can make its claims with all due certainty. Midwest folks are certain to continue taking cover when stormy skies turn an ominous green.

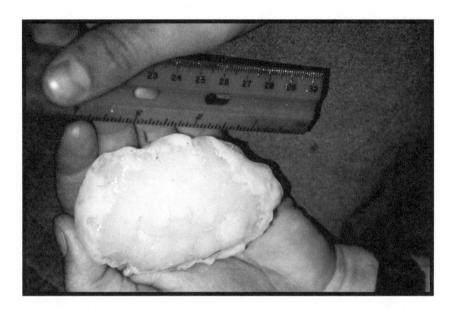

Golfers are especially at risk when large hail falls from the sky, as the duffers at St. Ann Golf Course found out in October 1984.

Hail Diameter

3 inches

Wind Gust

43 mph

Time and Location

October 8, 1984; St. Ann

1984: Hail Nails Golfers in St. Ann

October is often described as the best month of the year in Missouri. Nights are cool, and days are warm and dry. A fall sun illuminates the varied hues of the harvest season. Golfers enjoy the colors of woodsy buffers on each side of the fairways they play. Squirrels play, too. They scamper happily among all the acorns falling softly to the ground—much to the chattering creatures' delight.

October 8, 1984, should have been the kind of day to please chipmunk, woodchuck, and squirrel alike. It should have been a day of arcadian enjoyment for golfers making their rounds on the greens. However, the sun was not shining, and those were certainly not acorns falling from on high. What fell began as innocent and miniscule pea-sized mush balls. The grassy areas in St. Ann, a northwest suburb of St. Louis, began to disappear under a coating of white, mushy mothballs.

Golfers at St. Ann Golf Course must have joked that winter's worst had arrived early, shooing away any hint of Indian summer. Soon, though, the October storm was nothing at all to laugh about. Those frozen peas had grown to icy golf balls and were coming down hard and fast. Unhappy golfers began running frantically, trying to dodge an assault of hailstones that seemed to be growing larger—to the size of baseballs. Ouch! These huge globs of icy madness were inflicting much pain.

The daily *St. Louis Post-Dispatch* reported that many of the golfers took refuge in the course clubhouse. Ann McNicholas, who worked the snack bar at the St. Ann Golf Course, told the newspaper that on Monday, October 8, the golfers appeared beaten. She said several of the weather refugees had welts up and down their arms.

When lightning flashes, thunder growls, and hail threatens, an open golf course isn't the place to be. Large hailstones can be dangerous. A hailstone the size of a baseball can be delivered at the speed of 100 miles per hour. A strike on the head is much like getting beanballed in the major leagues.

Hailstones have caused death and serious injury in the United States, though the most lethal storms have occurred in other countries. In his weather study *Freaks of the Storm*, Randy Cerveny recounts the story of a 1930 hail event that killed twenty-two people in Greece. The deadliest storm was in India where stones the size of cricket balls ended the lives of 246.

The storm that ruined the golf day in St. Ann was part of a front that extended from Hannibal south to Ste. Genevieve. Upon exiting the area, the storm front left behind damaged cars, windows, roofs, and millions of dollars in insurance claims.

Hailstorms as intense as what hit St. Louis County are typical of April or May, not October. However, with the fickle weather of the Show Me State, all things are possible.

When a hailstorm begins delivering golf-ball-sized ice, it's time for all outdoor activity to come to an abrupt halt.

Hail Diameter

1.75–2.75 inches

Wind Gust

40–45 mph

Time and Location

April 10, 2001; St. Louis

2001: History's Costliest Hailstorm

"April is the cruelest month," declared T. S. Eliot in his 1922 epic masterpiece poem, *The Waste Land*. April of 2001 was both the cruelest and costliest month in Missouri, when the so-called "Tri-state Hailstorm" did more than $2 billion in damage across the Midwest. The series of raucous storms rolled in from eastern Kansas and brought mayhem to Missouri's I-70 corridor, then exited St. Louis for a final showdown in southwestern Illinois. At first, most of the concern was focused on the development of tornadoes.

One funnel cloud tracked along the I-70 corridor east of Columbia to St. Louis, although it caused negligible damage. Another tornado dropped out of skies in Callaway County, causing a fatality at a mobile-home site.

Although most meteorological attention was on tornado watches and warnings, the big event of April 10, 2001, turned out to be the monster hailstorm, which caused the most havoc in north St. Louis County. Almost every home and business in the area north of St. Louis City was damaged by hail. More than twenty planes at Lambert–St. Louis International Airport sustained damage. Flights were cancelled, and auto traffic in the area was brought to a standstill.

The suburban town of Florissant, otherwise known as the Valley of Flowers, was crushed by the storm, which hit about 8:30 p.m. Florissant mayor Robert Lowery said the hail seemed to start off as golf balls, which then grew to baseballs and softballs.

"It was a once-in-a-century event," said Lowery. "It was over within a half hour, but we were still dealing with the aftermath two years later. All the insurance companies dragged their feet on the homes, businesses, and auto claims. It was a nightmare." Insurance companies were accused of not honoring fair claims, of not even responding to claims, and of not paying full amounts for work required. The city of Florissant began providing its own damage inspections and assisted with claims and complaint forms.

Lowery said it was a battle to bring things back to how they were before the Tri-state Hailstorm. Forget that poetry of St. Louis native T. S. Eliot. Insurance adjusters in the St. Louis area needed no arguments from Eliot about April being the cruelest month after the 2001 spring hailstorm.

"If you were outside when that storm hit, there's no doubt you were in a life-threatening situation," said Mayor Lowery. "We had police go down after a couple of hail ball hits. It was torrential, and you could not see in it. You could not drive in it. We were unable to respond to calls. My advice to anybody who finds themselves outside in a storm like that is to seek shelter immediately. You can't wait to see if it will stop, or if it gets worse. When you are at Ground Zero in the Storm of the Century, it's time to take cover."

Hail is a familiar visitor to the Plains states that make up "Hail Alley," which does not include the state of Missouri.

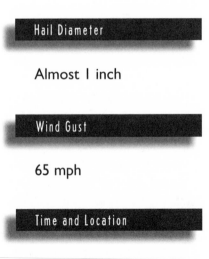

Hail Diameter

Almost 1 inch

Wind Gust

65 mph

Time and Location

July 14, 2007; Kansas City

2007: NICKEL AND DIMING KANSAS CITY

Kansas City gets its share of extreme weather, from below-zero cold snaps to sweltering heat waves. The great Missouri Cow Town has endured blinding winter snowstorms as well as noisy summer thunderstorms packed with hail and tornadic winds.

Nevertheless, Kansas City seems to never make the cuts for inclusion into the great geographic zones of dangerous weather. It's just outside of the infamous Tornado Alley, which runs north from the Texas Panhandle region through Oklahoma, Kansas, Nebraska, and the Dakotas.

Missouri's western metropolis also is well outside of Hail Alley, which takes in most of the same states as Tornado Alley, with the addition of eastern portions of New Mexico, Wyoming, and Colorado. Hail Alley gets its name for the frequency of the storms, as well as from the incredible size of the hailstones contained in many of its thunderstorms.

Kansas City certainly has a list of hailstorms on its weather resumé to make it a suitable applicant for inclusion in the hall of fame of Hail Alley. Missouri as a state has had a remarkable hail history, including many storms that piled up hail in a fashion resembling a winter snowstorm.

One humdinger hail event in the Kansas City area took place with a series of storms in the summer of 2007. Frontal boundaries will often remain stationary or move slowly during the summer months. Such was the case in July of 2007. On the Saturday evening of July 14, 2007, a cool front sagged south across eastern Kansas and western Missouri. The front may have sagged, but the weather it produced in the Kansas City area was no slouch. A series of storms blew up. Some were crawlers. Some were in a hurry. Northeast of Kansas City, quarter-size hail shredded leaves and winds clocked at fifty miles per hour brought down tree limbs.

A particularly strong storm raced south along the Missouri River from St. Joseph to Platte City to the north suburbs of Kansas City. Large hail was blown about by brisk winds. The winds chased out the early evening's stagnant summer heat.

The National Weather Service Forecast Office reported the strongest squalls passed right over Kansas City International Airport. Meteorological gauges at the city's airport recorded unusual fluctuations, including wind gusts of almost sixty-five miles per hour and temperature drops of close to thirty degrees. And, of course, there was plenty of hail described in size as nickels and dimes, quarters and half dollars. All coins from heaven were of the ice ball variety.

Kansas City's July 2007 hailstorm was notable, but nickels and dimes won't get you into Hail Alley. You probably need a hail boulder like they had in Coffeyville, Kansas, to make it to Alley status. It was 7.5-inches long and weighed close to two pounds!

Missouri has been hit by storm systems described as "inland hurricanes," and these weather complexes invariably deliver large, damaging hail.

Hail Diameter

I inch

Wind Gust

40 mph

Time and Location

8:15 AM on May 1, 2009; Reeds

In April 2009, the central region of the National Weather Service began using one-inch diameter hail as one of its new severe storm criteria. The standard for a severe storm rating previously was that it could deliver three-quarter-inch diameter hail. The new specifications for hail got a strenuous workout in forecasts and storm ratings in the very next month. Folks in the southwest Missouri town of Reeds saw little need to debate over the issue of whether they were, in fact, hammered by a severe storm.

Although the May 1 storm lasted only a matter of minutes after hitting at 8:15 a.m., it dumped enough hail to cover streets, yards, and roofs. The scene was downright wintry in a wide swath of southwest Missouri. Three hours after the storm's departure, plenty of melting hail was still on the ground on either side of Highway 37. Clouds of thick fog from evaporation hugged low areas of land. On rural side roads, tire treads left mushy tracks in the slushy remains of the long-gone storm.

Many of the hail balls surpassed the one-inch criteria for severe storm classification. More were ice pellets in a range below the revised measure for determining a severe storm. The new standard opened up a debate among weather spotters and spectators. Some argued that sheets of hail in the half-inch-diameter category, when blown by winds of forty miles per hour or more, could make for a pretty severe storm. Most meteorologists seemed to be on board with the National Weather Service's change on severe storm hail requirements. They clearly sought more of a focus on stronger storms.

Meteorologists argued that a lot of warnings about severe storms were like crying wolf too many times. All the crawl alerts on TV screens over harmless storms made for an inattentive, apathetic, and aloof public. Residents of Reeds were far from apathetic when hail from a morning supercell thunderstorm began to bombard their roofs. They said they were shocked by a driving rain of ice balls that interrupted their breakfasts.

"The worst of the storm was from Reeds north to Avilla," said Chief Tim Gunter of the Avilla Volunteer Fire District. "It was the biggest hailstorm we have ever seen—period. The roads were covered in hail; it looked like a snowstorm went through. Hail that was as big as baseballs did a job on vinyl siding and roofs. Our people saw back windows in cars busted out. It was a day of headaches for insurance adjusters."

Just a week later, another squall line slammed Reeds with wind and hail. It intensified as it headed east, dropping twisters in Springfield and in the Ozarks. By nightfall, the May 8 front was rolling into the Ohio River Valley. Forget severe storm labels, the AccuWeather forecasters at that point were describing the storm as an inland hurricane.

III. Floods

Floods in Missouri range from the nuisance variety to the catastrophic. Flash floods, which can become killers in a matter of minutes, occur on Ozark streams as well as on urban creeks swollen by the prodigious growth of shopping center pavement.

Major floods of some duration, which grow in intensity day by day, occur on the great rivers in the state, including, of course, the Mississippi and Missouri. Sometimes these two monsters go on a rampage and break through levees, causing unprecedented havoc while giving us unforgettable images of nature's wrath.

Most of the following section on Missouri floods was put together in 2008, a fortuitous time to be involved in such a project. As a newspaper journalist, I was flooded in 2008 with press advisories from agencies such as the National Weather Service, FEMA, the Red Cross, and the National Guard about an overabundance of water. Climatologists, environmentalists, and groups like American Rivers also chimed in.

"This is the second '500-year flood' in less than two decades, and the overwhelming scientific consensus is that climate change means more severe and more frequent storms, including more record-breaking floods," said Rebecca Wodder of American Rivers in a July 2008 statement. "Clearly business as usual won't work for the communities struggling to recover from this year's floods—and the communities at risk in the coming years."

Those of us who are lucky enough to reside on high ground in Missouri have witnessed numerous "100-year floods" and several "500-year floods" from a safe vantage point. Those who reside in low-lying areas of the state have endured the trauma of high water and the hardship after it recedes.

The 1993 flood figures prominently in Missouri history because it affected so many river towns. From Kansas City to St. Louis, from Canton to Cape Girardeau, the rivers made their angry presence known after weeks and weeks of torrential rains. Above St. Louis, the confluence of the Mississippi and Missouri rivers simply transformed into a giant lake. The Mississippi at St. Louis was fifty feet above flood stage for one hundred days. Residents marveled as the river crept up the steps to the Gateway Arch during the summer of 1993.

So many tales could be told about the flood of 1993—some were heroic, many were tragic, a few were just lowdown and despicable. The entire country learned about many of those stories as the national news media set up camp in Missouri. Peter Jennings, Tom Brokaw, and Dan Rather all came to cover the ordeal for the major television networks.

The flooding of 2008 also figures prominently in Missouri weather history. How could another 500-year flood hit the state in less than a score of years?

Actually, flooding in 2008 was even worse in neighboring Iowa. However, Iowa dispatched much of its water south to Missouri, which resulted in massive sandbagging efforts up and down the Mississippi. In Winfield, valiant efforts to shore up a levee failed, and burrowing muskrats were blamed for a calamitous breach.

Disastrous flooding also took place in the spring of 2008 on the state's meandering Meramec River. In late summer, freakish flooding throughout the St. Louis region came thanks to the remains of Hurricane Ike. Flash flooding by Ike on a Sunday morning caused millions of dollars in damage and several storm-related fatalities.

Floods not only impact residents' lives, they change the landscape, the geography, and the fate of towns and communities. Some residences and businesses in suburban St. Louis were abandoned forever after flash flooding from 2008's Hurricane Ike.

Reaching further back into the past, the Mississippi River flood of 1785 prompted a three-mile relocation of the town of Ste. Genevieve to its present site. The new site of the town was spared in 1993 only after more than 1 million sandbags were piled high to keep out the Mississippi.

The Missouri River and its history of bad flooding habits have certainly played a role in Kansas City's fate. Originally, a metropolis seemed destined to grow at the Wayne City Landing. The landing near Independence was a nexus for traffic on the Santa Fe Trail and a jump-off point for river commerce. A flood in 1844 pushed the site of the current city farther west.

Missouri river flooding also altered the character of Kansas City in the summer of 1951 after heavy rains in Kansas. Flooding did major harm to part of the pride of Kansas City—the stockyards. Business in the yards was never quite the same, and operations came virtually to an end within a few decades.

Torrential rains and the resulting floodwaters change history and influence the arts and culture of a people. News accounts, short stories, novels, and detailed histories are a part of the legacy of flood disasters. So, too, are paintings, murals, photographic documentation, and music.

Missouri's "larger-than-life" artist, Thomas Hart Benton, put his brush to work capturing nature's wrath on several occasions. Benton reveled in every detail of Missouri, and his home state's weather informed and inspired his creative genius.

Study the dramatic images of flood and storm that Benton committed to canvas, and you may find your inner ear bringing forth the mournful words and music of another art form:

"If it keeps on rainin', levee's goin' to break;
"If it keeps on rainin', levee's goin' to break;
"When the levee breaks, I'll have no place to stay . . ."

When the Mississippi River goes on a rampage, vast areas of Middle America can simply disappear for weeks.

The 1543 Mississippi River flood amazed Spanish explorers, who wrote that the river became a vast sea in many places.

River

Mississippi River

Year and Location

1543; Mississippi Basin

1543: The First Biblical Deluge

Since the arrival of the first white men to North America, there have been great "floods of biblical proportions." Devastating floods were a part of the lives and lore of Native Americans, but the Europeans brought the first biblical connotations to these catastrophic events. Many of these floods—with biblical effects rivaling the big event of Noah's time—occurred in the watersheds of the Missouri and Mississippi rivers. The liquid continental conflagrations amazed the new arrivals who most often did their exploring by boat.

One of the first recorded floods to hit what later became known as the Missouri region and the Louisiana Purchase came in the spring of 1543. A phenomenal Mississippi basin overflow coincided with the famous expedition of Hernando de Soto. The journey and flood were chronicled by the writer Garcilaso de la Vega, who described the flood as "of severe and prolonged duration." In fact, the flood had some biblical overtones in its numerology. It was recorded as beginning about March 10 with a crest forty days later. In other words, it was another one of those forty-day, forty-night affairs.

De Soto's expedition experienced the flood on the Mississippi River far south of St. Louis. In that locale, the river spread out over the delta region and transformed the entire area into a wide sea. From the perspective of the Spanish explorers, the flood must have brought to mind the great deluge detailed in the Book of Genesis.

Unlike Noah, however, de Soto was not charged with taking aboard representatives of all species of animal and bird in order to limit the loss of creation in the new land. Leaders of the expedition had their hands full with just keeping the Spanish troops alive in a territory of hostile natives and deadly natural hindrances.

Of the 1543 flood, de la Vega wrote: "Then God, our Lord, hindered the work [of the Spaniards] with a mighty flood of the great river, which . . . came down with an enormous increase of water, which in the beginning overflowed the wide level ground between the river and the cliffs."

The river extended nearly sixty miles across and eventually nothing could be seen except the tops of the tallest trees. De Soto is often credited as the European who first discovered the Mississippi, but he apparently did not himself encounter its mightiness as exhibited in the great flood of 1543. De Soto died in 1542 on the banks of the Mississippi. De Soto's men were said to have weighted and sunk his body in the middle of the river. They did not want the Native Americans to know that he was a mere mortal.

Many towns in the United States are named for Spain's great explorer, including De Soto, Missouri. A proud town that's had its share of nature's wrath, De Soto sits in the Mississippi River county named for Thomas Jefferson.

River towns of Missouri such as Ste. Genevieve have been battling floods since their inception and sometimes have even had to relocate.

Because of the troublesome flood of 1785, the French dubbed it *l'année de grandes eaux*, a.k.a. "the year of great waters."

River

Mississippi River

Year and Location

1785; Ste. Genevieve

1785: STE. GENEVIEVE UNDER WATER

After 250 years of persistent flooding, the drenched river town of Ste. Genevieve had reached the end of its rope. So in 1997, a colossal $40 million flood control project commenced involving 3.5 miles of levee, pump stations, concrete culverts, buried rail routes, sluice gates, and more. The project has been hailed as a water-control masterpiece—with its computer-controlled, fully automated hydraulic technology, and its massive, cutting-edge propellor pumps. Still, the skeptics point to floods as far back as 1785 and put their bets on the unbridled power of Mother Nature and peculiar antics of Old Man River.

Rising water from rains in the Mississippi basin brought destruction to the Ste. Genevieve area in 1973 and 1993. The flood of 1993 brought TV cameras from around the world to Ste. Genevieve. And why not? So much to focus on—thousands of tired volunteer sandbaggers, 1.1 million sandbags, 16,000 truckloads of rock, and $10 million in damage to the area.

Of course, long before modern man brought his technology to try to rope in the great river, Native Americans were coping with the Mississippi's maddening and mercurial behavior. Tribes moving about in this area of the Mississippi River Valley included the Quapaw, Shawnee, Delaware, Osage, and Kaskaskia. However, French colonialists are credited with bringing the first permanent, Western settlements to an area that became Missouri. One small village, established sometime before 1750, became Ste. Genevieve.

Old "Saint Gen" was one of several towns the French pioneers located in the southern regions of Missouri and Illinois. All of the settlements faced threats of flooding: Cahokia, Fort de Chartres, Kaskaskia, Prairie du Rocher, and Ste. Philippe. However, Ste. Genevieve, located in an amazingly fertile section of bottomland, was always the most vulnerable. That vulnerability became painfully apparent for the French settlement in 1785. Ste. Genevieve, named for the patron saint of Paris, confronted a much more unruly river than the Seine back in the old country. The river in this new country was uncivilized, untamed, and uncaring.

The Mississippi's bad manners spilled over in 1785. The French were forced to evacuate. From boats and from higher ground, they could see only the roofs of their cabin homes and trading posts. Water depths were estimated to be as high as fifteen feet. Lacking the wherewithal to build tall levees, pump stations, concrete culverts, and sluice gates, the French wisely retreated. They moved the remains of their town to a safer site three miles to the north.

The French came to call 1785 as *l'année de grandes eaux* or "the year of the great waters." Obviously, many such years of water followed at the new location of Ste. Genevieve.

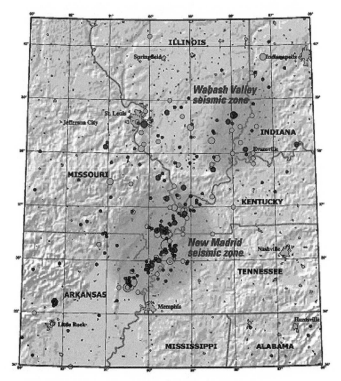

Scientists continue to worry about damage-prone river town and lowlands areas along the New Madrid fault.

The New Madrid earthquake caused fantastic flooding that would forever change the course of the Mississippi River.

River

Mississippi River

Year and Location

1811; New Madrid

1811: New Madrid Quake and Flood

Floods of biblical proportions are most often caused by forty days and forty nights of incessant rain. Flash floods occur all at once when it's "raining cats and dogs." The flood that took out New Madrid in the early 1800s was a little bit different in its origin. The swell of waters that consumed New Madrid did not originate with weeks of porous skies or cloudbursts. Rather, the flood responsible for the cataclysmic loss of fair New Madrid, Missouri, can be traced to a series of violent earthquakes, the worst ever to hit the North American continent.

The quakes began in the Missouri Bootheel on December 8, 1811, and continued for months. Most of the tremors were like ripples in a pond, but major temblors prompted the very ground to move like giant waves upon a wind-wracked ocean. Monster quakes along the New Madrid Fault, during the first three months of the apocalyptic event, split the earth wide open. Fantastic geysers of mud, sand, and carbonized wood erupted from the wetlands and lowlands of the Mississippi River.

The great river itself had its own catastrophic reaction to the rumbling along the fault. Riverbanks crumbled into its waters and were swept away. Towering shoreline cottonwoods and sycamores crashed into the waters, their trunks mixing with barns and houses in a stupendous vortex.

Obviously, the river mess played havoc with boatmen. In her account, *On Shaky Ground*, Norma Hayes Bagnall quotes eyewitnesses who were on the river. "The perpendicular banks, both above and below us, began to fall into the river in such vast masses," recalled an upset British traveler, John Bradbury.

At one point, the Mississippi was so dammed with debris it seemed to flow backward. The river changed course several times, and waterfalls were created upstream from the New Madrid settlement, much to the horror of its homeless residents.

Quakes caused the river to boil and heave. Water dissolved in lowland areas, then came back in twenty-foot walls that might have even shocked Moses. Great swaths of land did much the same thing: collapsing, rising, then sinking below the tumultuous waters. Such was the case with old New Madrid. Land sank, and a flood of water rushed over it at the Kentucky Bend. The town had to be rebuilt. Its location now is north of a riverbank created by the flood and earthquake.

In 1815, Congress came to the aid of those who lost so much with a "New Madrid Claims" law. Lost land from the disaster could be replaced with acreage elsewhere in Missouri. Critics charged that the government aid program was rife with fraud and abuse.

Those charges echo today's critics of relief programs. After all, they ask: If you choose to live next to a river, don't you accept the risk that a flood will come and take away all you own? Why should you receive aid for your foolishness?

Photos are hard to come by for the Great Flood of 1844, but more recent photographs of floods in the Kansas City region show the power of the area's rivers.

Factoid

This flood changed western Missouri's main port from one near Independence, Missouri, to what is now Westport, forever altering the location of Kansas City.

River

Kaw, Kansas, and Missouri rivers

Year and Location

1844; Kansas City region

1844: A Flood, a Trail, a City

Great Missouri floods have had a remarkable and sometimes nasty tendency to change lives, to alter history, and to rearrange local geography. This was true even before there were many lives to change in Missouri, much history to alter, or any significant plotted geography or maps to rearrange in the state.

An incredible flood in 1844 was a killer and surely a life-changer, but its effect was less than its potential because Missouri was sparsely populated at the time. Blame for the flood can be placed on heavy rains in Kansas falling every day in the late spring.

According to a history of Kansas by A. T. Andreas, the waters of the Kaw River rose high enough to put the west Kansas City area of Missouri under fourteen feet of water. The swollen Missouri River also piled its waters upon the Kansas City region. Bottomlands simply disappeared until a hot, dry summer replaced the exceptionally wet spring. The dead vegetable matter from the 1844 flood, decomposing under the scorching sun of a new summer, probably caused as much discomfort for the small population of the area as the seething spring waters.

Missouri weather wonks may be surprised to learn that the "Great Flood of 1844" was bigger in terms of cubic feet of water discharged than the more familiar catastrophic flood of 1993. The flood of 1993, however, caused more devastation because of a much larger population, more development, and levees producing higher river crests in the state.

By far the biggest impact of the 1844 flood was both geographic and historic. The great midcentury flood altered the flow of the Missouri River and created a rather troublesome sandbar in front of the Wayne City Landing at Independence. The sandbar ruined the landing as a jumping-off place for traders using the Santa Fe Trail, prompting them to instead use the Westport Landing in Kansas City. Thus, the 1844 flood had the unintended but salutory effect of encouraging the growth of Missouri's great western outpost of Kansas City.

Floods in Missouri often have had the surprising effect of altering landscapes and changing history. Farther downstream from Kansas City, the once-bustling village of Arrow Rock saw the Missouri River recede from below its bluffs and move almost out of sight of the historic town.

Even farther downstream, east to where the Missouri River pours its waters into the Mississippi, are more stories about the impact of floods upon local geography and history. Writer Mark Twain noted that floods have had curious effects, shortening and lengthening river passages, and throwing river towns out into rural districts. Floods, working in tandem with the fickle fingers of fate, gave state mapmakers new business.

Today's steel and concrete bridges are much better at withstanding floodwaters than the wooden structures in the Joplin area in the early 1900s.

Factoid

Shoal Creek feeds into Grand Falls, Missouri's widest, continuing natural waterfall and a Joplin tourist site.

River

Willow Branch Creek

Year and Location

1908; Joplin

1908: Clouds Burst Over Joplin

The regional metropolis of Joplin in southwest Missouri began as a tiny mining town, thanks to lead and zinc. The miners were a rowdy lot, and the town quickly earned a certain nefarious distinction for its ruffians, its saloons, and its gambling.

In the late 1800s, Joplin lacked the basics of law and order in a period that was described as its "Reign of Terror." Joplin's reputation wasn't helped a few decades later when outlaws Bonnie and Clyde took up residence there to rob banks and to kill several of the town's police officers.

In the middle of all this turmoil on the ground, there existed a kind of parallel lawlessness in the skies. Joplin sits at a crossroads of unstable meteorological activity. It sits in the crosshairs of nearby Tornado Alley and has somehow survived the worst of wind, rain, snow, sleet, hail, and more.

Now don't forget to add a few cloudbursts to the mix. One of the worst came in the spring of 1908. Rain descended in amounts difficult to describe or record. It was copious. It was most plentiful. It was abundant, ruinous, and overwhelming.

Words such as *cloudburst* should not be thrown around casually. The term is not exactly scientific in nature, but it does have some clearly definable characteristics. The mavens of meteorology note that it usually involves cumulonimbus clouds. These produce outrageously sized droplets of rain formed by the coagulation of many smaller droplets.

Before the meteorologists got hold of cloudbursts, the superstitious had their own ideas. They believed clouds were solid, balloon-like structures full of water. In especially violent storms, the balloons burst, ripped apart, and disgorged all their contents.

Anyway, let's get back to Joplin. On or around April 23, 1908, the town was shadowed by a wall of dark balloons, which burst and disgorged all their contents. A glorified creek called the Willow Branch, which flowed through Joplin's downtown, rose about fifteen feet in a mere half hour.

With this kind of hydrodynamic activity, it's not hard to imagine what happened to Joplin's many saloons, gambling joints, and room rentals of ruffians. Of course, the good people suffered as well. Newspaper reports tell of innocent young women in dry goods stores holding onto countertops and staircases for dear life.

Another way to imagine the 1908 cloudburst today is to head out of town. Travel a few minutes south of Joplin to where Shoal Creek becomes the widest and most scenic continuing waterfall in the state of Missouri. Joplin folks call this spigot of water their "Miniature Niagara Falls" and take pride in it. Imagine this Grand Falls flowing through the heart of downtown Joplin in 1908. It's sort of like what happens when a giant, dark water balloon rips apart over a town in the most violent storm imaginable.

St. Louis–area residents who live along the Mississippi's many tributaries will tell you that a canoe can sometimes come in handy during flooding.

The phrase "raining cats and dogs" probably can be traced to the major rains of England in the seventeenth/eighteenth centuries when animal carcasses would flow through the street with the rainwaters.

River

River des Peres

Year and Location

1915; St. Louis

1915: CATS AND DOGS FALL IN ST. LOUIS

In the rainy season in St. Louis, which can occur just about any time of the year, folks are heard to say that the rain is "really coming down"—or if it's a real gully washer, they will declare that it's "raining cats and dogs."

It's easy to be critical of the locals on the first count. Well, of course, the rain is "really coming down." It has no desire or propensity to travel upward. Sideways, maybe. But rain—through the ages—has always come down.

Rain coming down like "cats and dogs" is another kettle of fish entirely. But, even so, it's far more in the realm of possibility for rain to actually be coming down like a kettle of fish, than like a few cats or some dogs.

In the great weather book *Freaks of the Storm*, Randy Cerveny cites several instances in which it rained small fish in North America, South Africa, and Malaysia. However, for the purposes of this book, we must confine ourselves to talking about a downpour of felines and canines in the year 1915 in the city of St. Louis.

On a day in mid-August in 1915, St. Louisans were heard saying that it was "raining cats and dogs." Of course, in some neighborhoods, they were also heard saying—no, screaming: "Run for your life! Leave your house now!"

This is because six inches of rain had fallen in a very short time. The River des Peres was up to its usual no good in the central and southern parts of town. In fact, Mayor Henry W. Kiel ordered the street department to truck city harbor lifeboats to the Shrewsbury area and south.

The boats were used to snatch frantic residents from second-story windows of their homes. Firemen bound their waists with ropes tethered to trees before wading into swift waters to rescue stranded inhabitants in flooded St. Louis suburbs.

The *New York Times* referred to the storm as the heaviest downpour in St. Louis history. The *Times* told of a gusher of water entering the subway of Union Station through which rail baggage and mail was handled. Rail service into Union Station was halted, and passenger trains were stalled across the river in Illinois.

The 1915 St. Louis downpour had it origins as a killer hurricane that hit the Gulf Coast days earlier. Passing over the gulf from Cuba, the storm might have been expected to pick up some fish along the way. However, in St. Louis, the citizens were witnessing it rain like "cats and dogs."

So, where in the heck did the cats and dogs come from?

According to Gary Martin, otherwise known as "The Phrase Finder," Jonathan Swift gets the blame for the rain that brings cats and dogs to the Plains—or St. Louis, for that matter. The British writer wrote a satirical poem about a city shower: "Drown'd Puppies, stinking Sprats, all drench'd in Mud / Dead Cats and Turnip-Tops come tumbling down the Flood."

When the levee breaks, scenes like this result. The Great Flood of 1927 had a terrible impact from Missouri to far south Louisiana.

This massive flood stretched across seven different states, caused $400 million in damage, and killed 246 people.

Mississippi River

1927; southern Missouri

1927: Levee-Breaking Torrents

"If it keeps on rainin,' levee's goin' to break;
"If it keeps on rainin,' levee's goin' to break;
"When the levee breaks I'll have no place to stay..."

Led Zeppelin has given us many musical ballads that have agitated, excited, and inspired us. None of the ballads compare in simplicity—and yet in sheer, haunting repetitiveness—as the Zep's incredible 1971 ballad "When the Levee Breaks." Few Zep fans could know that the song actually originates with the husband and wife blues team known as Kansas Joe McCoy and Memphis Minnie. The two recorded the music and lyrics in heartfelt response to the Great Mississippi Flood of 1927, which had a terrible impact on seven states from Missouri to far south Louisiana.

The flood was a yearlong ordeal that began in the summer of 1926 when heavy rains swelled tributaries in Kansas, Iowa, and Missouri. By May 1927, the Mississippi River grew sixty miles wide south of Memphis. Almost a sixth of Arkansas was lost under its muddy waters. The great 1927 deluge should be much more prominent in American history for three reasons: its awesome magnitude; its effect on race relations and racial migration; and its impact on culture as manifested in folklore and music from folk and blues, to rock.

In magnitude, the 1927 flood must be classified in a category by itself. Hundreds were drowned; thousands were displaced. Levees began breaching in Missouri, and by the time the conflagration was over, more than 140 levees collapsed up and down the length of the Mississippi River. Almost 350,000 African Americans lost their homes, and many were forced to work at gunpoint, for no pay, to shore up levees in flood relief efforts. In the flood's aftermath, a great migration of African Americans commenced to cities of the North, from St. Louis to Chicago to Detroit.

What the rich man's history left unrecorded, the poor man's memory captured in mournful song. Bessie Smith, Lonnie Johnson, Barbecue Bob, and many more put the flood in their music. Robert Plant adapted music for Zeppelin from Joe McCoy and Memphis Minnie. The English rock group recorded the revised song at a faster tempo, then engineered it down to create the song's eerie tonal landscape. Zep's indefatigable drummer John Bonham pounded away at his drums, while a harmonica wailed away like a building storm. Zeppelin's song is one for the ages—as was the Flood of 1927—and the song and its theme got a workout in 2005 with a hurricane called Katrina. Once again, there was the evil of the water and a sad indifference to the plight of the poor and minorities.

"Cryin' won't help you, prayin' won't do you no good;
"When the levee breaks, mama, you got to move."

Shack homes in Illinois, Kentucky, and the Missouri Bootheel went under water in the terrible winter flooding of 1937.

Factoid

Pioneer John Hardeman Walker fought for the inclusion of the Bootheel in Missouri's border upon upon realizing that, otherwise, some of his land would straddle state lines.

River

Mississippi and St. Francis rivers

Year and Location

1937; Bootheel

1937: Bootheel Lost to Flooding

Missouri was almost deprived of its "Bootheel" when the state was first under consideration for joining the Union. Its southern border was to be a straight line, east to west, like the separation of Kentucky and Tennessee.

A pioneer planter named John Hardeman Walker didn't cotton to the idea of a straight-line border. He also insisted the counties of Dunklin, New Madrid, and Pemiscot did not belong in the Arkansas Territory but instead in his Missouri. His logic about this heel-shaped floodplain between the St. Francis and Mississippi rivers held sway with the federal authorities.

Missouri got its Bootheel, but this land, which Walker won for the state in 1821, was stolen for a time by cruel nature in the harsh winter of 1937. The raging St. Francis and Mississippi rivers conspired to take huge swaths of land, as well as many of the lives of citizens in southeast Missouri.

A mix of rain, snow, and ice pelted the Midwest for weeks before all the great rivers and tributaries groaned "enough" of the storms' loads. On the west side of the Bootheel, the St. Francis and Black rivers breached levees and scoured a score of towns from Kennett to Senath to Red Onion and on down to Arkansas.

Trouble heaped even higher on the Bootheel's east side, because the swollen Ohio River emptied its load into an already angry Mississippi. Newspapers throughout the country chronicled the woes of Charleston, Sikeston, East Prairie, New Madrid, Caruthersville, and more.

In Missouri's capital of Jefferson City, legislators debated over how much aid should be appropriated. A ten-inch snowstorm, drifting outside the doors of the statehouse on January 22, seemed to emphasize the emergency happening in the state. "It is the duty of the legislature, with the snow falling, to take speedy action to care for the people of the state in need of relief, if the need exists. This is no time to quibble," State Senator J. S. Rollins of Columbia told his fellow legislators.

Hundreds of tents and supplies were sent downstate for relief camps established on high ground. Red Cross volunteers warned farmers to leave their lowland homes or face "drowning like rats." Never mind all those pitiful drownings; soon the bitter cold, food shortages, and spreading typhoid began to take their toll.

Henry McLemore, a writer for the United Press, reported on the six hundred refugees lucky enough to make it to high ground in Caruthersville: "I listened to them tell of their frantic exodus from the bottomland shacks when the Mississippi surged over its banks to become a death stream 23 miles wide."

"More are struggling in each hour," McLemore continued. "They represent the ultimate in poverty. They had nothing before this flood. Now they have less."

The Kansas City stockyards sprawled along the city's river bottoms area, which went under water in the massive flooding of 1951.

Factoid

The Kansas City stockyards were once among the largest in the world, second only to the Union Stockyards of Chicago.

River

Kansas and Missouri rivers

Year and Location

1951; Kansas City region

1951: Kansas City Stockyards Flood

Kansas Citians will chafe, bristle, and moan when their cosmopolitan city is described as just a "cow town." Royals baseball fans get particularly upset when their town gets tagged as a cow town by impolite visitors, such as uppity St. Louis Cardinals fans. There was a time, however, when Kansas Citians were proud to live in a cow town. They bragged about it. They built monuments, sculptures, and plaques to Hereford bulls. Some even insisted that mechanical bull rides were a Kansas City invention.

Where does all this bull come from? Well, the facts are that Kansas City once was a "cow town" with one of the largest stockyards in the world. Established in 1871, the Kansas City Stockyards by 1900 were second only to Chicago as a prime destination for millions of heads of cattle, sheep, hogs, mules, and horses.

The stockyards grew up along the Kansas River, conveniently located near the Kansas and Missouri Pacific Railroad tracks. The stockyards were claimed by two states, with two-thirds of the yards in Kansas and one-third straddling the Show Me State.

Kansas City's stockyard operations hit their peak in the 1940s, but in 1951 a great flood of epic proportions smashed through the West Bottoms area where the Kansas River meets up with the wide Missouri. The yards, slaughterhouses, and meat-packing businesses were bludgeoned by the crush of water and never recovered.

The flooding began in June 1951, when the skies opened up in western Kansas from Manhattan to Topeka to Lawrence. July only got worse. In one five-day period, beginning July 9, a foot and a half of rain fell in Jayhawk locations. All that water headed east, topping levees, with much of it funneling into Kansas City's stockyards area at the confluence of the Kansas and Missouri rivers.

According to the National Oceanic and Atmospheric Administration, the worst day was July 13. The Kansas River and its tributaries all seemed to crest on the 13th. In Missouri and Kansas more than 2 million acres of land were flooded. Rivers stayed above flood stage for weeks.

Kansas City was not the only big loser from the midcentury flooding. Missouri residents had to evacuate from Boonville to Jefferson City, from Hermann to St. Charles. Total damage to Kansas and Missouri was in the billions in today's numbers. The damage to Kansas City could not be measured simply in casualties or dollars and cents. The flood did irreparable harm to part of the pride of Kansas City—the stockyards. The business in the yards was never quite the same, and operations finally ended within a few decades in 1991.

Kansas Citians need not flee their "cow town" heritage. They might even revel in their past—maybe over a Kansas City strip steak. Remember the stockyards—and the Flood of '51!

Brush Creek adds ambiance to Kansas City's Country Club
Plaza, except when it goes on a flooding rampage, as in
September 1977.

Factoid

The largest Missouri Civil War battle, the Battle of Westport,
was fought on either side of Brush Creek in Kansas City.

River

Brush Creek

Year and Location

1977; Kansas City

1977: Bulletin from Brush Creek

Every Thanksgiving night, the big switch is thrown and holiday lights in Kansas City's Country Club Plaza go on—all at once. The spectacle draws thousands, as shiny bulbs accentuate every tower and dome in the Spanish-style entertainment district. The tradition has been carried out since 1930 and is as loved as the songs of Christmas carolers and the clippety-clop of horse-drawn carriages in the ornate plaza. Work to prepare the countless strings of lights often begins in later summer, and the takedown can last into March.

In 1977, the great tradition of the lights was almost snuffed out. In fact, the entire plaza itself was put in peril by a tiny stream that turned into a monster. Heavy rainfall in September 1977 drove Brush Creek crazy and sent it tearing through the heart of the beloved Plaza area.

Long before the area at Broadway and Ward Parkway was even settled, nearby Brush Creek had a bad reputation for mercurial behavior. Early farmers noted that it was hard to find—covered with brush most of the time—and that it was notably infested with water moccasins. If you couldn't find Brush Creek in the dry summers of nineteenth-century Kansas City, there was every chance the "creek" would find you during fall and spring downpours. This prompted several efforts at flood control, including a pave job by notorious political boss Tom Pendergast, who used his own concrete company for the task.

The paving of the creek was good for a lot of folklore about buried thugs and innocents, but for flood control—not so good. That became evident after sixteen inches of rain hit the Kansas City area on September 12, 1977. The small stream, flowing between the popular plaza and a row of fashionable high-rise apartments, suddenly became a river—and then a great lake.

Kathy and Randy Hartman, transplants to Kansas City from St. Louis, loved living in those tall apartments, while dining and working in nearby Country Club Plaza. Randy had a job in a plaza office with no windows, so he was not alarmed when his worried spouse, Kathy, called him again and again about the overflowing creek. Randy did not see what the fuss was all about, but he finally took heed when his wife yelled into the phone: "If you don't get out of that building, you are going to die!"

Twenty-five people did die. Daring rescues saved motorists, while their cars simply floated away. Plaza businesses were inundated by ugly water, and then left covered with mud and silt. Raging Brush Creek did almost $100 million in damage to the gemstone of living and shopping in Kansas City. Even so, plaza proprietors cleaned up and insisted on getting lights back up in time for Christmas. And the Hartmans cheered when warm lights on Thanksgiving night, 1977, shone past the bad memories of Brush Creek's September indiscretions.

Bluffs on either side of the Jacks Fork River contribute to
its tendency to flash flood, as in the deadly storm event of
January 1982.

Jacks Fork's rapids place it in a Class I–II floating category.
However, dangerous weather situations may place it in a
more perilous category.

River

Jacks Fork

Year and Location

1982; Eminence

1982: Jacks Fork's Deadly Flash Flood

illie Plowman of Eminence was working the dispatcher's desk for the Shannon County sheriff when the call came in: Two young men from the St. Louis area were likely in a heap of trouble on one of the rivers. Terry J. Grissom, twenty-four, and his buddy Christopher M. McCarter, twenty-one, had asked a canoe operator to trailer them to the upper Jacks Fork for a winter canoe and camping trip. It was late January, and the trailer driver warned them that thunderstorms were in the weekend forecast.

The two canoeists got more than just thunderstorms on that Saturday of January 30, 1982. They got heavy rain, sleet, thundersnow, and blizzard conditions. They also got flash flooding, which always antagonizes the rivers and streams in the Mark Twain National Forest of Missouri. "I was raised in the canoe industry and my dad ran a rental operation in Alley Spring," said Robin Brewer of Circle B Cottage Cabins in Eminence. "My daddy always said you don't mess with Mother Nature on rivers when storms are coming. I was young when that tragedy happened, but everyone around here knows about it."

Chris Brewer, Robin's husband, operates Windy's Canoes & Tubes in Eminence. He said it was a nice day when another operator dropped the two canoeists off at the Highway 17 Bridge just east of Buck Hollow.

"It's theorized that they woke up late in the night and found several inches of water in their tent, and they tried to walk out to civilization," said Chris Brewer. "That time of year, they should have been camping on higher ground and near an access point. They weren't prepared for the worst."

Dispatcher Plowman recalled that roads were blocked with snowdrifts. The weather was so cold and icy that an airplane was sent up to find the young men. The canoes were spotted near Chalk Bluff Hole. "The search party found one fellow frozen to death in what we call Iron Stake country on the Tuesday," said Chris Brewer. "The other fellow had walked about three miles up around Chalk Bluff and froze up against a cliff. The Park Service does its best to find people in trouble, but when you're in a blizzard and a flash flood, it's not going to work out too well."

Lillie Plowman, who was born in Alley Holler on the Jacks Fork, said lots of folks volunteered to walk into the snowy forest to find the lost men. "That was the biggest river tragedy we ever had that didn't involve some murders," said Plowman. "That was just the worst time to be out there. Everybody got involved: the sheriff's department, the park service, the highway patrol's plane was sent up.

"Those two guys had their own canoes, but they probably shouldn't have been trailered in there," said Plowman. "People insist they know what they are doing, but what do you do up against a flood and a blizzard?"

After 1982's floods, the cleanup of contaminated Times Beach cost millions.

Because Times Beach was built on the Meramec River's floodplain, its first buildings were elevated on stilts.

Meramec River

1982; Times Beach, Valley Park, and Kirkwood

1982: OUTRAGE AT TIMES BEACH

Stormy weather in 1982 was particularly scary for Missouri communities along the muddy Meramec River, especially for those downstream from a very muddy town known as Times Beach. That's because Times Beach was thoroughly contaminated with a carcinogen known as dioxin.

When heavy rains began to hit the eastern Missouri area in December, folks started asking if all that dioxin was getting into their drinking water. Dioxin was spread in the small river hamlet of Times Beach when a fellow named Bliss was contracted to spray waste oil on its roads in dry seasons. Bliss's waste oil helped keep the dust down when cars drove on the unpaved roads. Only problem: Bliss had mixed dioxin waste with the oil to make it stretch farther—not a great idea for the health of humans, pets, and wildlife living in the area.

On the night of December 14, heavy rain and tornadic winds hit the town of Kirkwood. The freak storm took off roofs and snapped twenty-seven utility poles. Francis Scheidegger, the city councilman for Kirkwood in charge of public safety, worried about the strain on the city's electric workers as they tried to put the electric system back together.

As more December storms rolled through, Scheidegger began worrying about his town's drinking water. The rising waters of the Meramec flooded Kirkwood's water plant. Scheidegger began wondering about that dioxin from Times Beach. The water plant drew water from the Meramec River Valley, so was dioxin getting into the residents' water supply?

Scheidegger and others in St. Louis County began making a lot of noise about the problem. State officials said the Times Beach dioxin was not water soluble and, in any case, was probably being filtered out by water plants. Even if that could be believed, it was alarming to learn that floodwaters were spreading the dangerous material all over areas in St. Louis County.

In December 1982, the flooding Meramec covered Times Beach with ten feet of water, chasing out 95 percent of the residents. In January of 1983, the Environmental Protection Agency (EPA) noted that the dioxin levels in Times Beach were one hundred times higher than the level considered safe for humans, and it resolved to chase out all the residents with a $32 million buyout.

Even with the town evacuated, something had to be done with all the dioxin-contaminated soil. Plans to shove it all into a mountain bunker were shot down, because the unruly Meramec would be too close to the toxic mountain. So, millions were spent to burn the deadly dirt.

Today, Times Beach is now called Route 66 State Park. EPA officials insist all the dioxin is gone. One thing that's not gone is the Meramec River, which periodically rolls and roils and overflows its banks—showing that nature's rage is not easily contained.

Floods not only damage outdoor recreation areas, but also they can be lethal in underground recreational caves in Missouri.

Because of caves' many sinkholes and penetrable limestone, they become especially dangerous during high waters.

River

Mississippi River

Year and Location

1993; Cliff Cave in St. Louis

1993: Cliff Cave Flash Flood

Cliff Cave south of the Jefferson Barracks Bridge in St. Louis has a haunted history. Once known as "Indian Cave," the bluff-side cranny reportedly was a refuge for Native Americans as long ago as 7000 B.C. Much later, the cave was a hideout for thieves and pirates who hijacked unsuspecting travelers on the nearby Mississippi River. In Civil War times, it was a rendezvous for Confederates who hatched plans against the forces of the Union upriver in St. Louis. Cliff Cave later acquired a notorious reputation as a bivouac for illegal booze and mobsters during the violent Prohibition period in America. At various times, the cave has been a haunt for those who've trucked in theft of life and property.

Given its larcenous legacy, Cliff Cave was no place to be in 1993 when the swollen Mississippi River went on a rampage not far from the cave. That summer of 1993, St. Louis skies often opened up every afternoon to add more insult to the swollen river.

A group of five children and two counselors from the St. Joseph's Home for Boys showed up to explore the cave on the afternoon of July 23, 1993. The roadway into the cave area was blocked, but any danger was not apparent to the young entourage.

Local cave experts explain that at the back of Cliff Cave there are two sinkholes that drain runoff from the subdivisions built on the bluffs above the Mississippi. When it storms, all the runoff goes straight down the sinkholes and into the cave below. When pounding rains began to drain into Cliff Cave on July 23, the would-be explorers became trapped. No one could get to them as the skies opened up and the cave flooded with runoff water. In the end, everyone but a thirteen-year-old boy drowned. The young teen crawled up onto a high ledge in the cavern and stayed put until the water receded.

Many tragic stories flowed from the 1993 Midwest floods, but none involved as many fatalities as the ill-fated adventure at Cliff Cave. Despite its deadly legacy, seasoned cavers defend Cliff Cave. TThey argue the 1993 tragedy was a consequence of extreme weather conditions and poorly drained new development in a nearby area, not because the river cave itself is inherently dangerous.

After the deadly calamity, a long investigation followed. Surviving family members wanted the cave closed for good. The St. Louis Parks and Recreation Department asked for cavers' input on that idea. Based in part on their feedback, the cave has been placed on a permit system for any future exploration. A gate at the cave has only been partially successful in stopping new adventurers— young folks who may not know the story of the Cliff Cave drownings. Perhaps the site needs a memorial marker to all the cave's flash-flood fatalities of 1993.

Sandbagging efforts to protect a home or community involve back-breaking work, and anyone who sabotages such efforts can expect reprisals.

James Scott is the only person to be charged and convicted for "causing a catastrophe" in state judicial history.

Mississippi River

1993; Marion County

1993: WEST QUINCY CATASTROPHE

I n the infamous summer of 1993, Mother Nature intentionally caused a catastrophe. She unleashed a train of thunderstorms that piled up water, day after day, in the Mississippi River basin. When the water took its course south to the Gulf of Mexico, it became a destroyer without a conscience. Destruction did not take place all at once or in any one locale. There were multiple acts of perdition. In Missouri, it was another ride of the James Gang. The destruction could be described as excessive, widespread, wanton, senseless—almost criminal.

Who might be tried for 1993's high-water crimes and Mississippi misdemeanors? You can't indict a Madame of Nature. You can't arrest and hold a river for trial— even when the guilt is obvious all over its muddy face.

In Marion County, Missouri, upset residents wanted justice and revenge. The angry citizens found a poor fellow to try for the watery assault on their properties. The name of the alleged miscreant: Jimmy Scott.

Water broke through the levee at West Quincy in Marion County on the evening of July 16, 1993. Within a matter of hours, the river created a lake of twenty square miles and ten feet deep. The bridge connecting Missouri flatland to the bluff town of Quincy, Illinois, was put under water.

Jimmy Scott, twenty-three, an employee of Burger King in Quincy, became the prime suspect as word spread that the levee may have been sabotaged. For one thing, Scott had been seen walking alone near the dam break shortly before it gave way. He was by himself, while others were furiously sandbagging to prevent a disaster. For another thing, Scott had been heard bragging that he would break the levee to maroon his wife on the Illinois side. With his wife stranded, Scott could freely drink and carouse with other women in Missouri.

Scott was tried twice and found guilty twice. After his second trial, the judge spoke for the people who were swamped by the flood: "I can't take your property as you took theirs, but I can take your liberty, which I hope that as you have time to contemplate, you will find is more precious."

Adam Pitluk, author of *Damned to Eternity*, chronicles the strange case of Jimmy Scott, the first man in history to be arrested, charged, tried, convicted, and sentenced to life under the obscure state statute of intentionally causing a catastrophe. Pitluk suggests there are as many holes in the Scott case as there were leaks in the river levees in 1993. He also emphasizes Scott's plea of innocence and a lamentably long sentence.

St. Louis Post-Dispatch reviewer Harry Levins takes issue with Pitluk and writes that Scott was a low-life scoundrel of minimum wage days and maximum beer nights. Levins declares author Pitluk to be green and gullible and cites the ironic adage: "There are no guilty people in prisons. Just ask 'em."

St. Louis riverfront attractions shuttered during the Flood of 1993, but that was a minor part of the story, as water rose closer to the legs of the Gateway Arch.

Factoid

As the worst flood disaster since the Flood of 1927, the Great Flood of 1993 caused $15 billion in damage, and at least thirty-two lives were lost.

River

Mississippi and Missouri rivers and River des Peres

Year and Location

1993; St. Louis and the River Valley

1993: Telegenic 500-Year Flood

Accounts of misery and heartache swirled out of the floodwaters. They spilled barrels of ink onto newsprint in the great 500-year flood of 1993. Storm and flood headlines grabbed the attention of the Show Me State, the river valley region, and an entire nation. News media arrived from world capitals to cover the deluge. There were so many stories of loss to cover.

Veteran television journalist Don Marsh of St. Louis rates the big flood as a story for the record books, both in impact and for its sheer duration. The Mississippi River was fifty feet above flood stage for one hundred days. With forty thousand square miles soaking under water, damage exceeded $15 billion. No price could be tagged on the wrenching emotional cost of the 1993 disaster. That's the primary reason, Marsh says, that the big flood brought an unmistakable message for his profession. It read: "Made for Television."

For farmers, the emotional "Made for TV" moment came when levees broke and farm homes were swept off their foundations. Houses, barns, and silos bobbed in the tsunami like bathtub toys, then split apart and splintered into pieces. TV stations went live.

For suburban business owners, the emotional "Made for TV" moment came when the only way to get to work was by rowboat. In Chesterfield Valley, the flooding Missouri River went wild—put the interstate under fifteen feet of water and swallowed businesses whole. TV stations went live.

For city folks, the emotional "Made for TV" moment arrived when the Mississippi River backed up into the St. Louis tributary known as the River des Peres. Suddenly, residents were in a water war and sandbagging for dear life to save their homes. When they lost the battle to save their neighborhoods, TV stations went live.

For rural folks, emotional "Made for TV" moments came when their hometowns went totally under water. Families hugged, clutched grab bags of salvaged belongings, and wondered aloud as to where they might spend the night. TV stations went live.

Don Marsh, a dean of St. Louis broadcasting, pronounced the 1993 coverage as one of the exemplary epochs of local television news. Great stories and images were provided of heroic people coping, fighting, surviving—winning against tough odds. However, when the floodwaters finally receded, and the dramatic pictures were gone, Marsh laments that TV news did not cover the big issues left in the mud and mold and debris. What should happen next? "Rebuild homes? Rebuild levees? Let the rivers take back what rightfully belonged to them along the floodplain?" Marsh asks in his memoir *Flash Frames*. Buyouts? Bailouts? In many ways the story after the flood was as significant as the flood itself. That story was important, but not so dramatic. So, the TV stations went elsewhere.

Muddy waters of the Missouri River cover bottomlands almost every spring, but in 1993 and 1995, those waters covered roads, railroad tracks, and river towns.

Factoid

Despite its vulnerability to unpleasant flooding, Hermann has won the coveted title of Missouri's Most Beautiful Town for multiple years.

River

Missouri River

Year and Location

1995; Hermann

1995: Muddy Missouri v. Maifest

After weeks of spring rain, folks in Missouri began to wonder in May 1995 whether they were facing a repeat performance of the disastrous flood of 1993. As Yogi Berra would say: It was deja vu all over again from St. Louis to Kansas City. TV weather forecasters once again spoke of flood stages and crest predictions. Radio stations blared news of road closings and car rescues. Photos of sandbaggers and houses under water anchored the front pages of the state's newspapers. Banner headlines proclaimed: "Here We Go Again."

Residents of the town of Hermann, safely ensconced on their high bluff, looked north over a vast lake that was once Missouri River bottomland. The tiny towns nestled along the bluffs opposite Hermann were under cold, murky water the color of mud.

Although most of Hermann was safe from the flooding, its annual outdoor party known as Maifest was not spared. Wine country's grapes went unshared. Glasses failed to twinkle with the reds and whites of previous harvests. Maifest was canceled. Travel to Hermann, a quaint town sometimes referred to as the capital of wine country, was far too treacherous. From some parts of the state, the trip was simply impossible. Water flowed over rural roads and state highways.

The Flood of '93 put a damper on wine country traditions and was a blow to the tourist economy of towns like Hermann. However, the harmful ways of the flood were much worse for towns whose homes and businesses sank below river waters.

Show Me State citizens soon began asking: How could a 500-year flood, like the tsunami of 1993, be repeated in Missouri once again after only two years? How could it actually be worse than the 1993 deluge in many areas? *Missouri Conservationist* writer Jim Auckley noted that levee repairs and precautions taken after the 1993 flood made things worse in the 1995 flood. A new "mega-levee" designed to protect one town simply made things worse for a town farther up the river.

Auckley quoted Norm Stucky, an environmental coordinator with the Missouri Conservation Department, about his take on the return of the big flood. Flood damage in some locations in 1995 was actually worse than two years earlier. "There have been five major floods on the Missouri River in the last 20 years," explained Stucky. "Now 20 percent less water gives us a six-foot higher stage—the floodplain is so restricted that the river no longer has the natural capacity to handle floods."

Despite all this, urban developers and industrial site builders have continued to gobble up cheap river bottomland for commercial uses. After 1993 and 1995's devastation, can we persist in the folly of "trying to conquer so mighty a resource, when floods and destruction are the result?" was the question posed by Auckley.

Johnson's Shut-Ins was devastated by the dramatic flood of December 2005 after the collapse of the AmerenUE reservoir that was used to generate electricity.

Factoid

After being closed since the catastrophe, the state park re-opened in May 2006 with limited access. Swimming was still prohibited as of summer 2009.

River

Black River

Year and Location

2005; Johnson's Shut-Ins

2005: Taum Sauk Reservoir Flood

Johnson's Shut-Ins has forever been prized as one of the most magical of natural locales in the Show Me State. Massive boulders, colorful rocks, and swift waters combine to form chutes, slides, and cascades. The state's parks department has referred to this unique stretch of the Black River flowing through shut-ins as a "Nature's Waterpark." The rocky natural formations have energized active youngsters and simply awed their more sedentary elders.

On a dark December morning in 2005, the magic at Johnson's Shut-Ins was literally washed away; the colorful rock was submerged in thick mud, grime, and heavy silt; nature's waterpark became a man-made mess. A tall wall of water, some twenty to thirty feet high, raced down nearby Proffit Mountain and totally flooded the shut-ins.

A large breach in the AmerenUE hydroelectric dam atop the mountain allowed 1.5 billion gallons of water to rush downward. A "fail-safe" device, designed to prevent reservoir overfilling, malfunctioned big time. Some anxious utility employees had reportedly warned of potential problems.

The failure of a 650-foot section of dam was more than a problem for Jerry Toops and his young family. The superintendent for Johnson's Shut-Ins Park instinctively knew what was wrong when his park home virtually exploded at five in the morning from a tsunami-like crush of cold water. He soon found himself swimming upward—ten feet, twenty feet, then thirty feet before surfacing. He told William M. Hendryx in a *Reader's Digest* account that there was no time to try to reach his wife, Lisa, or their three children. While clinging to a tree in the flood, he was certain they perished, and he blamed himself for their deaths.

Jerry Toops was found about an hour after the water crested. Clinging to the upper limbs of a tree, Toops was bleeding and in shock. A party of nine rescuers trudged through hip-deep mud and the added insult of a light snow to find the survivors. Members of Toops's family were found, scattered like so much driftwood in the mud, but they were discovered alive.

"If not for these nine men, acting fast in the dark, frozen moments after the flood, one, some, or all of these five lives would have been lost," noted U.S. Representative Jo Ann Emerson in a February 1, 2006, speech. "They are heroes. They responded without hesitation and we owe them a debt of gratitude. I commend them today in the U.S. House of Representatives, and thank God for their great deeds."

The Taum Sauk flood stands out as an exception in this book, because it was not really a natural disaster. It was man-made and could have been averted with care and due diligence. However, the incident at Taum Sauk may well stand out as the most potent example of nature's wrath when man attempts to dramatically alter her landscape for his own purposes.

A late winter flood in 2008 forced many residents of Meramec River Valley towns to abandon their homes.

Factoid

During the spring 2008 Midwest flooding, the Meramec River crested fifteen feet above flood stage in some towns.

River

Meramec River

Year and Location

2008; Pacific, Fenton, Arnold, Eureka

2008: Gawkers Along the Meramec

Flood gawkers! Who are they? Are they insensitive voyeurs who delight in the misfortunes of others? Or, are they just naturally curious humans who empathize with folks in the midst of trouble and travail? In 2008, Missouri offered plenty of weather events for gawkers—and for those wishing to study the behavior of gawkers. The year was the wettest in state climatological history. Rains came in amounts that far surpassed the Great Flood year of 1993. And so, 2008 became a good year for gawkers. However, police, fire, and rescue workers were spurred to issue warnings for gawkers to cool it—to stay home or to keep moving when in the vicinity of disaster areas.

During March of 2008, the bloated Meramec River in eastern Missouri provided "a gawkers' paradise" from west of Pacific, through Fenton, past the town of Arnold, and far along to where the Meramec's waters finally empty into the Mississippi.

In Pacific, gawkers stood on high ground and watched scores of homes and businesses get swamped by rising waters. They watched sandbaggers work to save the three-story Great Pacific Coffee Company.

Nearby in Eureka, gawkers caught sight of dirty water creeping into the subdivision of Emerald Forest. At Eureka High School, the baseball backstops were underwater and field equipment was set adrift.

Farther downstream, gawkers took in the view from Interstate 44 near Valley Park. Chocolate waters were climbing up to the bridge deck of I-44, a place where the Meramec already had submerged the crucial county artery of Highway 141.

A few miles to the southeast, gawkers gazed at the tops of street signs in old town Fenton. The landmark Joe Clark's Restaurant was an island in the Meramec, precariously protected by a wall of sandbags on all sides.

Before the Old Gravois Bridge was declared off limits, gawkers stood on the bridge just east of Joe Clark's and watched debris race by below in the Meramec channel. Propane tanks, bottles, furniture, matresses, old and new appliances, abandoned boats—all raced by at breakneck speed on a route to the Mississippi River. Missouri Highway Patrol Sergeant Julie Scerine had a warning for the gawkers: Get too close to the waters and you could be joining all that goo and debris. Scerine stressed that the shoulders of roads and highways were for emergency stopping only—not for sightseeing stops.

How many traffic accidents near the flooded areas could be traced to gawking, Scerine couldn't tell the press precisely. However, she knew they were happening with alarming frequency in Missouri's flooded areas. "Nobody wants to cause car accidents, but at the same time, this is a unique experience," came a gawker's defense of his gawking habit.

Winfield residents can be stoic about floodwaters entering their river town, but they get angry if a levee break is caused by negligence or a pesky muskrat.

The Winfield levee breach of 2008 was 150 feet wide.

Mississippi River

2008; Winfield

2008: MUSKRAT MISCHIEF AT WINFIELD

B efore two songsters oddly named Captain & Tennille came crooning, coital habits of muskrats were likely of interest only to naturalists and conservation agents. Captain & Tennille's top-of-the-charts ditty about the amorous antics of two furry little creatures changed all that.

Their curious lyrics about Muskrat Sam and Muskrat Sue were accompanied by synthesizer interludes. The noises were meant to mimic the chatter and swooning of muskrat foreplay. The muskrat song made it big. ". . . Now he's ticklin' her fancy/ Rubbin' her toes/ Muzzle to muzzle, now anything goes/ As they wiggle, and Sue starts to giggle . . ."

Rural folks who know muskrats have to wonder just how up close and personal Captain & Tennille got to the pesky varmints. After all, they fall into the category of aquatic rodents. Folks in Winfield, Missouri, find little amusement in any muskrat behavior, amorous or otherwise. In fact, there's no love lost between the average Winfielder and your average muskrat. Blame those hard feelings on the Mississippi River Flood of 2008, when Sam and Sue's wiggling poked holes into the Pin Oak levee.

Muskrat burrows on the riverside of the levee caused the Pin Oak to sag and then collapse, and water rushed over thousands of acres of land in the Winfield area above St. Charles. An additional wall of sandbags could not hold the water back, and one hundred homes were inundated by a wall of water.

Newspapers across America told the story of how the Missouri critters turned an earthen stronghold into a soggy mush. In the nation's capital, the *Washington Times* ran a news account with an accusatory headline: "Muskrat destroys Missouri levee."

A few newspaper stories hinted that the guilty muskrats of Winfield were finally captured by the National Guard and were subsequently not treated so kindly. Missouri game laws allow the trapping and shooting of muskrats considered culpable in property damage cases.

Of course, Winfield's muskrats had their defenders as well. Some argued the musky burrowers were not the dirty rats they were made out to be! If they did cause the Pin Oak levee collapse, then they performed a service by easing flooding downstream in Old Monroe and St. Charles in Missouri and at Grafton and Alton in Illinois. Others, testifying in defense of the muskrats, argued that the slandered rodents don't dig deep enough to bring down a properly constructed dam or levee. Pinning blame for the Pin Oak demise on poor muskrats was simply an exercise in scapegoating at a time of stress and anger in Winfield.

Whether muskrats can ever beat the rap for flooding Winfield in June 2008 is doubtful. One thing is for sure, no one in Winfield will be caught "singing and jinging the jango" about muskrat love. No, not any time soon.

Hurricane Ike's remains hit St. Louis in September 2008, flooding homes, apartments, and businesses near urban streams.

2008: Hurricane Ike's Flash Flood

It was no secret that a major storm—Hurricane Ike in a previous life—was on its way to St. Louis. When it hit, however, no one was prepared for the kind of flash flooding it unleashed in the Gateway City on the Sunday morning of September 14, 2008.

Ike was the worst hurricane of the season to hit the North American continent in 2008. Ike devastated Galveston and the Texas coast. Ike persisted in its deadly ways far inland into the states of the Old Confederacy. Still, no one expected the storm to maintain a deadly punch by the time it hit the Midwest metropolis of St. Louis in eastern Missouri. Hurricanes aren't supposed to hit the heartland. That's what Colleen Reany thought.

Reany awoke at 9:30 a.m., September 14, to the thunderous noise of a retaining wall collapsing at her Brentwood apartment complex. Within seconds, her first-floor apartment began to fill with water. She and her roommate had only enough time to put on shoes and climb through a window to safety

Many residents of the Manchester Road area, west of the St. Louis city limits, had similar escape stories. The nearby Deer Creek and Black Creek went out of control due to downpours from the remnants of Ike. The flash flooding in suburbia put motorists on Manchester Road at risk, and several dramatic rescues were required.

Austin Sherill, a Webster Groves High School senior, rescued a woman from her stalled vehicle. Floodwaters were up to the middle of the windows of the panicked woman's Honda CRV. Inside the car, the water was up to her waist.

"The water was moving swiftly, and the car was being swept away," Sherill recounted. "She popped the door open and gave me her hand. I grabbed it and pulled her out. As soon as she stepped out, she went straight down and into the water."

By holding onto a telephone pole, Sherill was able to drag her out of the deep. Moments later, the CRV was swept off in Deer Creek's raging water, which seemed determined to dump into River des Peres on the St. Louis city border.

Stephens Floor Covering, Gibson Carpeting, Parties and Props, Roehm Brothers Construction, Roesel Tire, and Auto Center all sustained heavy flood damage. Trainwreck Saloon on Manchester Road was under water, as was Rock Hill Lumber Co. Boards and wood panels broke away and floated east.

Cousin Hugo's bar and restaurant went under water. Later in the day, Cousin Hugo's owner, Tommy Bahn, waded through the shambles: "It's devastating. We've never experienced anything of this nature."

David Wilson, an environmental expert with the East-West Council of Governments, said the area could expect more of the same in the future. Wilson said overbuilding in a watershed area that was once a floodplain was a formula for flash flood disaster.

IV. Blizzards and Ice Storms

Winter storm warnings used to be all about snow. A potential blizzard was on the way. Smiles came to the faces of kids, as they hoped for school closings and sled rides on a neighborhood hill. Adults shared in the mirth, but worry also set in over grocery supplies and the whereabouts of melting salt and the snow shovel.

Winter storm warnings now, all too often, seem to be about a "wintry mixture" of freezing rain, sleet, and snow. A potential ice storm is on the way. Kids still hope for school closings, but they have no use for ice. Adults worry whether a coating of ice will bring power outages, injurious falls, and the loss of that favorite backyard tree. Ice storms are ubiquitous in Missouri. No residents are spared. Every corner of the state has taken a turn coping with its "ice storm of the century," although the Interstate 44 corridor from Joplin to St. Louis has been brutalized extraordinarily often by ice-filled terror.

Kansas City has certainly had its share of ice storm havoc. The western Missouri metropolis has winced and withered in icy weather madness in 1996, 2002, and 2003. Freezing rain and sleet brought misery from Crown Center and the Plaza to the suburbs of Independence and Olathe.

No one feels the brunt of ice storms worse than utility repair crews. In the Kansas City area's 2002 nightmare, hundreds of linemen were out in numbing cold trying to restore power. Their biggest fears were "hangers"—trees and limbs perilously close to falling on wires undergoing repair.

Joplin and Springfield were visited by the evil iceman in 2006 and 2007. Joplin meteorologist Gary Bandy speculates that global warming may be a culprit in an increase in ice storms. Atmospheric layers of warm air are turning what used to be snowstorms into devastating and costly freezing rain and ice events.

The impact of ice storms is both physical and mental, as Springfield's Kirk Hansen of Fantastic Caverns will attest: "We will remember the depression that set in. Everywhere you looked—a huge mess. A time to rest or just hang out didn't exist— just endless problems to be solved." Hansen tells tales of his younger brother who had a small generator. Relatives without power took up residence in his home along with "indoor" dogs, cats, and other itinerant pets. After twelve days, Hansen said his poor brother was muttering about braving the cold to "dig a few shallow graves."

Eastern Missourians endured ice, cold, treacherous travel, and darkened homes in 2006 and 2009. The storm of 2006, which ravaged St. Louis, resulted in fatalities from residents trying to stay warm with indoor charcoal and kerosene fires. Carbon monoxide poisoning emergencies were common. In the aftermath of the storm, the electric utility, AmerenUE, and Saint Louis University launched a joint project to install one hundred computerized weather stations to monitor service area conditions. The system will give the utility the "eyes and ears" to know where line disruptions are most likely to occur in future dangerous weather events.

The 2009 ice storm did its worst work in southeast Missouri. A newly elected U.S. president declared the region a disaster area. Hundreds of state residents were put up in temporary shelters from the Bootheel and Sikeston north to Cape Girardeau. Although the 2009 ice storm was a monster, it's hard to know if citizens of Cape would trade it for the snowstorm of 1979. Snowstorms are not usually as destructive as ice storms, unless they're like the 1979 blizzard that hit Cape Girardeau with fifty mile-per-hour wind gusts and drifts up to six feet.

Three things stand out about Cape's 1979 storm: The snow's intensity was a complete surprise; it hit in a freakish narrow band; it was accompanied by lightning and thunder. "It was such a very localized event, which our retired weather guy still can't live down," said Cape meteorologist Brian Alworth of KFVS-12 TV.

There is something that stands out about many of Missouri's all-time record snow events—quite often they are characterized by "thundersnow." The incredible 1982 blizzard in St. Louis was likened to a long train of one summer-like thunderstorm after another—only the precipitation was not rain. It was wet snow piling more than two feet high. Baby boomers who lived through the thundersnow of January 1982 will be telling their grandkids and great grandkids about the storm that shut down their city for days. It was a quirk storm, but one for the record books.

Columbia had its own "freak show" thundersnow in December 2006. As with the great St. Louis storm twenty-four years earlier, the snow fell at record rates. Columbia forecasters saw this one coming, but the weather folks still were amazed as bolts of blue lightning and loud cracks of thunder were a part of near white-out conditions.

Seven decades earlier, another memorable storm hit the Columbia and Jefferson City area. Newspapers in January 1937 were full of news about horrible weather plaguing Missouri livestock that were freezing to death up in Kirksville; fatal car accidents in snow north of Jeff City; and flood and frostbite casualties in the Bootheel.

Even so, the *Daily Capital News* found space in the paper for a little happy news about the deep snowfall. Its story revealed the antics of grownups using bobsleds and sleighs on closed city streets. The story's front-page headline proclaimed: "Snow Brings Back Childhood to Adults."

Extended blizzards and ice storms can be particularly hard on livestock, as was the case in central Missouri in the winter of 1937.

Amount of Snow

10–12 inches

Date and Location

January 22, 1937; Jefferson City

1937: Old Man Winter in Jeff City

O ld Man Winter set up camp in Jefferson City and throughout central Missouri in the first three months of 1937. From Kirksville to Columbia on to the state capital, the blustery old fart brought ice and sleet, unprecedented snow totals, and record cold.

Kirksville endured several cold waves that kept temperatures near zero for days. A thick coating of ice caused heavy livestock losses, both from loss of pasture and from accidents involving falls on the slick surface.

From Macon to Columbia, roads were often impassable and closed. When they reopened after plowing, they were still icy and treacherous. Autos slid into ditches and stayed put for several days until wreckers with wenches and cables could get to them.

Jefferson City was hit by the worst sleet storm in memory the week of January 10. Over the next two weeks, Jeff City suffered a one-two punch of snowstorms bringing near-blizzard conditions to much of central Missouri.

One benefit of the snowstorms was that it kept the state legislators off the streets. They were locked up in the chambers of the statehouse debating a number of critical issues. Some of those serious concerns had to do with another kind of weather—torrential rains and flooding.

While southwest Missouri was dealing with rain, sleet, accumulating ice, and thundersnow, the southeast region of the state was coping with incessant rain and severe flooding. The Bootheel area was under water. Thousands of residents in a portion of Missouri known as "swampeast" were living in makeshift tent camps.

With huge snowflakes swirling around the capitol dome, Governor Lloyd C. Stark told legislators about the need to address a flood emergency in the Bootheel. As many as fifty thousand families were in need of relief.

The ice and snow outside made it hard for legislators to fathom a rushing flood many miles southeast of the cold, snowy capitol. The daily *Jefferson City Post-Tribune* reported that Senator Joseph Brogan of St. Louis introduced several resolutions granting relief. A bid of $950,000 for a three-month relief effort was deemed too much by some legislators and entirely "too modest" by others.

Not everybody was consumed by the state's crisis flooding or the state's ice and snow emergency. Both young-at-heart adults and their children made their way onto the hilly streets of Jefferson City with their Christmas sleds, bobsleds, and skis delivered by Santa in December.

Police roped off streets near the capitol for the fun. They warned any motorists to steer clear. "Tumbles were frequent, but without harmful results," reported the *Daily Capital News*. "The snow was deep and soft. Older people joined in the fun, holding their own sleigh-riding and sledding parties," the paper noted. "Some had sleigh bells that served to add to the merriment."

Snowstorms can leave a Winter Wonderland in their wake, but they put a terrible strain on emergency repair services before their departure.

Amount of Snow

24–30 inches

Date and Location

February 25, 1979; Cape Girardeau and southeastern Missouri

1979: BLIZZARD OF CAPE GIRARDEAU

Snowstorms spread all across the Midwest in January 1979. Three feet of snow piled up in areas from Kansas to Indiana and north into Wisconsin. Temperatures plunged well below zero, and some counties simply turned into blocks of ice.

By far, the freakiest storm of the 1979 winter season occurred at the end of February in a small patch of southeast Missouri. The area hit took in towns like Chaffee, Delta, Oran, and the river city of Cape Girardeau. What started as a mild rainstorm ended with Governor Joseph Teasdale declaring the region of the state as a bona fide disaster area.

The soft rain began on a Saturday evening and grew more steady as the clock struck midnight. Lightning and thunder arrived with a shift in the wind out of the north. Temperatures dropped like a rock, and by morning towns along Interstate 55 were being buried by a thundersnow event. Visibility dropped to only a few yards by late morning and snow depths were at two feet and more. Drifts grew to five and six feet as howling winds were clocked as high as fifty miles per hour with gusts. All traffic was brought to a standstill, and motorists were stranded on the interstate.

By Tuesday, Cape's daily newspaper was full of stories of emergency operations, rescues, and traffic bans. A headline in the *Southeast Missourian* declared: "Say Nothing More About Snow of 1917–18." The yardstick for measuring great snows in the future would be the blizzard of February 25, 1979.

The *Missourian* chided weather forecasters who had predicted two inches of snow for Sunday. By late Monday, some cars had disappeared under snowdrifts of eight feet. The Missouri National Guard arrived that Monday, and helicopters were enlisted to assist with medical emergencies in rural areas without electricity. "Cities banned traffic, and travel was allowed only by permit," recalled TV weather forecaster Bob Reeves of KFVS-12 TV in Cape Girardeau. "We were fortunate at the station to have two of those permits.

"Snow was over the tops of the parking meters downtown along Broadway, and there was nowhere to go with it," recalled Reeves. "The snow plowed off the parking lots was piled in huge mounds that really did not completely disappear until May. It's the only time I ever saw a snowdrift at my home more than five feet against my patio door."

In the "Blizzard of '79," hotels were packed along I-55 on a stretch just south of Sikeston to north of Cape Girardeau. Weary travelers showed up at hotel doors and were barely able to walk from exhaustion. The *Missourian* reported that Ramada Inn employees could not make it to work, so visiting Rotarians picked up the slack. They waited tables, made beds, mopped the floors, and poured much-needed coffee.

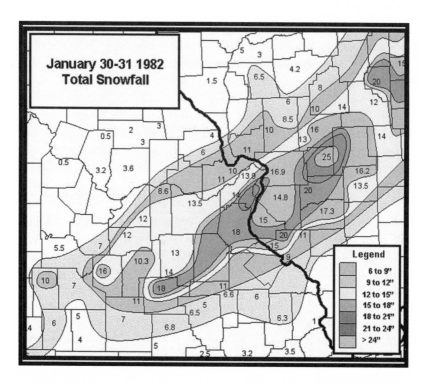

A narrow band of snow at the end of January 1982 paralyzed the St. Louis area, closing schools and businesses for almost a week.

Amount of Snow

25+ inches

Date and Location

January 30, 1982; St. Louis

1982: Thundersnow Buries St. Louis

Sometimes a snowstorm can grow unusually angry. Snow clouds will reflect strange flashes of light, and the thunder will growl. Wet snow usually piles up in unprecedented amounts when the sky puts on such a display. Such was the case in the early evening of Saturday, January 30, 1982, in St. Louis, when huge raindrops morphed into giant snowflakes. By midnight, those flakes were racing down at the rate of an inch per hour, and they were periodically illuminated by nature's flash bulb—lightning.

Veteran TV meteorologist Dave Murray calls the 1982 storm the most quirky weather event of his years of forecasting in St. Louis. It was the winter storm of a lifetime with a record snowfall for a twenty-four-hour period. "The Blizzard of 1982 was a true thundersnow," recalled Murray. "In a very short period of time, we picked up as much as twenty-five inches of snow. Thunderstorm cells of snow kept training over St. Louis, but sixty miles east and sixty miles west of the St. Louis area—hardly any snow at all."

Some parts of St. Louis received 25 inches of the white stuff, which would have made it the worst blizzard of all time. However, the official measure at the National Weather Service was about 14 inches, which meant it fell short of two storms: a 20-inch snow in 1890 and a 15.5-inch snow in 1912.

A *St. Louis Post-Dispatch* editorial criticized the Weather Service measurement at Lambert Airport for only catching two of every three snowflakes that fell. The editorial noted an odd "barrage of thunder" heralding the record storm. "The very magnitude of the blizzard may have held down the loss of life that always accompanies a bad winter storm, although thirteen deaths were attributed to it," declared the *Post*. "When the snow totals nearly two feet, there is a powerful, life-saving incentive against trying to dig your way out of Siberia."

Out in the suburbs, piles of snow paralyzed cities without equipment to deal with such massive amounts. In Webster Groves, three of the city's six snowplows broke down. City trucks were enlisted to become police cars. Ambulances stalled in snowdrifts, and firemen were called upon to take Terri Beilstein to the hospital when she went into labor at 5:45 a.m. on January 31. The Webster Groves woman gave birth to a seven-pound, nine-ounce baby boy. Brian Eric came into the world on the heels of an epic thundersnow.

The storm was given credit nine months later for an unusual spike in the number of babies showing up in maternity wards. Thundersnow and lightning! Snowbound couples apparently found ways to pass the time.

Thundersnows, like the great St. Louis storm, inspired a study at the University of Missouri, funded by the National Science Foundation, into the "when" and "why" of such freakish weather phenomena. How, indeed, do these concentrated blizzards happen?

Temperature is the key to whether a winter storm brings heavy snow or a thick coating of ice.

18 inches

December 1, 2006; Columbia

2006: COLUMBIA'S "+" SIGN SNOWCAST

S nowstorms in the Midwest, and especially in Missouri, are difficult to predict. A difference in temperature of a degree or two can mean the difference between a coating of sleet or a thick blanket of snow. The way a low-pressure system bobbles on its path from west to east can mean the difference between a few snow-flakes and blizzard conditions. The timing of wind shifts and the wind's velocity can be crucial in the impact of a snowstorm.

A week before the big snowstorm dump of December 1, 2006, most mid-Missouri forecasters were pretty sure they were looking at a major weather event taking shape. The stars were aligning. All the essential ingredients were present. And there was a certain magic in the air.

Josh deBerge, then a meteorologist at KOMU-TV in Columbia, started to get excited about what seemed to be coming together on Sunday, November 26, al-most a week before the first flakes would descend in his forecast area. First of all, computer models indicated a deep low-pressure system and secondary low head-ing to the middle of the country. Add to that a jet max over the area, increased divergence aloft, and a TROWAL. Together they equaled trouble. That TROWAL is an acronym for a Trough Of Warm Air aLoft, for the uninitiated. Weather wonk deBerge said it all meant the sky could wring out lots of precipitation. "By Wednes-day, we were mentioning snow totals as high as twelve inches for Friday morning," said deBerge. "I recall some intense discussion over whether we should add a "+" sign to the forecast to indicate higher amounts were possible. We did."

Meteorologist Eric Aldrich and deBerge upped the snow prediction and kept the "+" on Thursday morning. However, the precipitation came in as sleet, con-tinued as sleet, and showed no hint of any change to snow late Thursday night. "I dozed off to sleep fully expecting a fairly large forecast bust. The layer of warm air aloft would not cool, and our changeover to snow would not happen," KOMU's deBerge recalled.

About 1 a.m., the young Columbia forecaster woke up to a sharp crack muffled just enough for him to know that it was thundersnow. He jumped to the window to see heavy snow falling with four or five inches already on the ground. With the dawn, snow rates were at two to three inches per hour.

"What I remember about the storm the most is the incredible lightning," said deBerge. "There were at least ten cloud-to-ground lightning strikes with loud cracks of thunder during my morning commute all in near white-out conditions. By the time the snow ended, we measured eighteen inches in the studio parking lot," noted deBerge. "It was a record snowfall for the day and close to a record for a twenty-four-hour snowfall."

An active winter weather season in 2008 was probably not a surprise to Ozark folks who watched the forecast signs in persimmons, holly berries, and bushy caterpillars.

Amount of Snow

8 inches

Date and Location

March 4, 2008; Ozark County

2008: Ozark Persimmon's Snow Prediction

Two distinct bands of heavy snow snaked their way past the southern border of Missouri and through Ozark country on March 4, 2008. One band stretched from West Plains to Rolla, while another narrow column covered Cassville to Jefferson City. These corridors of snowfall brought amounts ranging from four to eight inches or more. Most of the snow fell in the morning hours at rates of as much as three inches per hour. The quick accumulations were as much of a surprise to observers as the quirkiness of the two separate storm paths, which were roughly parallel.

This was a memorable Missouri winter season that came in with a December ice storm and marched out with several impressive snowfalls. Oh yeah, and don't forget to throw an unheard-of number of winter tornadoes into the weird weather mix.

Ozark folks, who looked earlier in 2007 for the many signs that nature provides for forecasting weather, may have been less than surprised by the active winter of 2008. First of all, there are those creepy caterpillars, referenced as the wooly worms by those in the prognosticating business. Wooly worm watchers will divide into two camps. Some say a thick wool coat reveals harsh months ahead, while others refer to an orange band on the critters. A wide band of orange points to a milder winter.

Then, there are cornhusks to reckon with. Thick husks to protect the corn seeds suggest a colder winter with plenty of precipitation.

When oaks produce a lot of acorns in early fall, it's time to prepare for the worst. The number of acorns that cover the circumference of a tree in the final week of September gives more than an inkling of the ink that will be devoted to major snowfalls in future press accounts.

How about those holly berries? If the bushes are weighted down with clumps of berries around harvest time, then best be prepared for the coming of a new ice age.

Another sure winter predictor, relied upon in the Ozarks, is the old persnickety persimmon's seed. The fruit itself grows on a tree and looks like an orange tomato. Inside is the mysterious seed that reveals all.

"It's a cherished bit of Ozarks folklore that the shape of the tiny seedling can predict conditions in the upcoming winter," said Patrick Byers, a University of Missouri Extension Service horticulture specialist. According to the persimmon's lore, a fork shape on the seed signals a mild, warmer-than-average winter; a spoon shape indicates above-average snowfall; and a knife shape means bitter, cutting cold is on the way.

Show Me State residents recoil in horror at nature's wrath, but it's not as if they aren't given fair warning. They just need to check out acorns, berries, cornhusks, and those wooly worms trying to cross the road.

Rime ice tends to be less destructive and more decorative, while glazing in ice storms disrupts lives with accidents and power blackouts.

After the power outages in 1987's ice storm, the Ozark electricity provider, Ozark Electric Cooperative, committed $10 million in system improvements.

January 1987; the Ozarks

1987: Glaze v. Rime in the Ozarks

When winter's ice storms hit the Missouri Ozarks, residents hope for a lighter kind of freezing rain, the kind that leaves the beauty of rime ice, rather than a dangerous glazing.

Ice storms of any duration usually coat everything with a layer of frozen precipitation. The coat thickens as more freezing rain falls and becomes a hard, glass-like glaze. This sort of heavy storm causes major problems.

A less intense storm of light freezing rain, drizzle, and fog can bring the magic of rime ice and can provide aesthetic delight. Soft rime provides a sugary coating of ice crystals that seem to stick together like tiny pieces of hard rock candy.

When rime ice paints the rolling forests of the Ozarks, the landscape becomes enchanted. Trees, both small and tall, glisten with a sticky dust of powdered sugar. Branches on firs and evergreens bend with the weight of feathery white stuff in a virtual kaleidoscope of design. Fallen foliage no longer looks like cast-off debris. Crinkly brown leaves transform into translucent pendants—nature's very own costume jewelry. Weed shoots and brush become glittery, comb-like structures. Together, they all point reverently away from frigid gusts of wind.

In January 1987, Ozark residents braced themselves when weather forecasters issued winter storm advisories for ice and snow. They hoped to dodge the worst of it. Perhaps the heaviest weather would pass to the south in Arkansas, and Missouri could be treated to drizzle, fog, and a feathery coat of rime ice. Nature was having none of that. Ice glazed roads, bridges, trees, power lines, and poles with a heavy two-inch coating. Schools closed as roads iced. Cars collided. Trucks crashed. Power towers collapsed. The lights went out for almost a week.

Ozarkians pronounced the weather event as at least as bad as the ice that hit in the early 1970s. And the glaze of ice hung around, especially at higher elevations. South of the Missouri Ozarks, heavy rains flooded Arkansas residents out of their homes.

In Missouri, the problem was cold and darkened homes. When a falling tree landed on a wire, weight on the other side of a pole would sometimes snap the wire. The scenario repeated itself across the Ozark hill country. Repair crews with ice cleats on their feet, and with layered clothing to fight off the cold, took on electric jobs that would be routine on normal days. In the aftermath of the 1987 ice storm, Ozark Electric Cooperative committed $10 million to clear power line right-of-ways of trees and foliage to prevent a repeat of 1987.

Glazing ice storms in the Ozarks bring most life to a standstill. Is it an Ice Princess or an evil Mr. Freeze that puts everything in its glaze? One thing is for sure, these storms are without rime or reason.

As the icicle teeth of a winter storm grow longer and heavier, they begin doing costly damage to homes and businesses.

Kansas City's severe ice storm of 2002 left 270,000 residences without power and kept utility repair crews busy for days.

January 29–30, 2002; Kansas City

2002: Kansas City's "Perty Ice Storm"

Mixed emotions can result when the "Winds of Thor" blow in a wintry mix of cold rain, freezing rain, sleet, and ice. That's because the unique effects of ice storms can be at once beautiful and dangerous, brilliant and hazardous. Such was the case on January 29–30, 2002, when a slow-moving storm arrived in Kansas City and western Missouri. The winter squall covered everything in its path with a heavy coat of sparkling ice. What a remarkable transformation of an otherwise drab winter landscape was wrought by nature's hand.

An almost divine artistry could be discerned in tiny nooks and crannies, as well as in wide country vistas. The translucent pigment was composed of freezing rain, which remained liquid, until it splashed upon a sprawling canvas and froze on impact. House gutters became glistening gums anchoring rows of icicle teeth. Shingle rows on sloped roofs became wavy, shiny slides. Sidewalks turned into slick, foreboding paths. Streets turned into perilous ice rinks.

In abandoned gardens, browned and withered long-stemmed shoots became icy stems for crystal goblet glasses. Sculpted evergreens opened up to the skies and spread their icy wings wide like some novel, varied form of Venus Flytraps.

Conifers were in all their glory. Nature dressed them up in genuine Christmas tree garments. Tall oaks chose to accept their weighty ice blankets, while old elms and young fruit trees groaned and snapped at their unwanted icy burdens.

So much for all the brilliance and beauty. There was a price to pay for this dazzling wonderland. Highway traffic snarled. Shaky pedestrians toppled. Hospital rooms filled. Power poles snapped. Homes went dark. Hapless humans shivered. Frozen tree limbs crashed across electric wires and tore meter housings from residences. More than 400,000 homes and businesses were without power. Utility repair crews and pole jockeys worked 24-7 with wires, sockets, meters, transformers, ties, and wraps to try to restore the power. "I didn't know what day it was. When you don't go home, you just don't know," Temple Electric's Mark Gauldin told *Electrical Wholesaling* magazine in a wrap-up article titled "Kansas City's Icy Nightmare."

Utility experts pronounced the ice storm a once-in-a-century event for Kansas City. Dallas-based Temple Electric and firms from all over the country assisted three hundred electric utility repair crews on the job from Kansas City Power and Electric.

A presidential disaster declaration cleared the way for millions of dollars in recovery assistance. Add "costly" to such derogatory adjectives as "dangerous" in describing the Kansas City Ice Storm of 2002. But, oh, what an astonishing spectacle it was!

Ice storms not only glaze paths to front doors, but also obstruct sidewalks with fallen trees and tree limbs.

Southeast Missouri's 2006 ice storm introduced a month of December in which fifteen weather records would be broken in the state.

Date and Location

November 22–December 1, 2006; Joplin

2006: JOPLIN'S EARLY WINTER ICE STORM

When you live in Joplin, Missouri, it may be hard to imagine that you will soon feel the atmospheric effects of what's happening in the Rockies or in Alberta, Canada. In mid-November of 2006, that is precisely where Joplin's weather was being made. Moist air from the Gulf of Mexico also got in on the action. The storm system out of the Rockies pulled up the Gulf moisture from the south, but the back end of the storm pulled down the cold air out of Canada. The result was a pool of cruel and unusual weather that lasted from about November 22 through December 1.

Joplin meteorologist Gary Bandy at KSN16-TV watched it all unfold with fascination. It began with severe thunderstorms and temperatures in the seventies. Act two consisted of several days of freezing rain, ice, and sleet. The final act involved heavy snow tracking into central Missouri, where some snow bands dumped as much as seventeen inches of the white stuff.

According to Bandy, the ice storm portion was especially debilitating, as tens of thousands of residents in southeast Missouri lost power. The worst of it came on November 29–30 when surface temperatures fell below freezing, but a layer of warm air over southeast Missouri insured that the precipitation fell as freezing rain rather than snow.

"Winter precipitation is the most difficult to predict," Bandy explained. "When an ice crystal falls out of a cloud in June, it will fall as rain. If it falls out of a cloud in the winter, it may arrive as rain, freezing rain, snow, or sleet. When the ice crystal falls out of the cloud and encounters a layer of warmer-than-freezing air, it melts," Bandy continued. "But if it then falls through a layer of freezing air, it will re-freeze, resulting in ice and possible ice storms. You can see it all coming on radar, but accuracy on the type of precipitation can be tough. That's because most of the freezing action occurs in the vertical plane."

The ice storm of late 2006 was just the first in a series of unusually harsh ice storms that hit Missouri in the latter part of the first decade of a new century. These storms resulted in millions of dollars of damage, power outages, loss of work and school days, and injuries and deaths on the road.

"Interestingly enough, yet counterintuitively enough, these ice storms are yet another clue that our climate is warming," Bandy said. "Ice storms do not generally occur without a layer of warmer-than-freezing air in the middle atmosphere. Were the atmospheric column completely below freezing from the cloud base to the ground, these storms would have been significant, but not devastating, snowstorms. Ice storms such as these used to be prevalent in central Arkansas and points south, but they have been migrating north recently."

Roads in St. Louis County became impassable because of
downed trees in the ice storm of 2006.

More than half a million homes were left without power in
2006 after an intense ice storm in the St. Louis region.

November 30, 2006; St. Louis

2006: Ice Attack on St. Louis Tree Cities

The Big Bad Weather Wolf huffed and puffed for a couple of memorable storms in 2006 in St. Louis. He may not have blown many houses down, but he sure did manage to turn off the lights. He knocked out the power.

The Gateway City's first encounter with the cantankerous canid came on July 19. His eighty mile-per-hour winds knocked out electricity for more than a half-million people in the midst of a summer heat wave. Tempers grew short with the power company, AmerenUE.

The wily wolf came back to taunt the town on November 30 with sleet and ice. Trees full of ice crashed to the ground and dragged everything down with them, including power lines. More than a half-million people lost electricity again. When teeth weren't chattering, they were bared in anger once again at the power companies, which struggled to get lights—and heat—back on.

Power outages were widespread in many St. Louis suburbs designated as Tree City USA locations, including Kirkwood, Webster Groves, and more. All those maples, birches, ashes, pears, redbuds, and dogwoods were perfect for Arbor Day Foundation awards, but fared less well on November 30. When the Big Bad Weather Wolf came to town, the trees came down. They split at their forks and cracked at their crotches. They toppled from their trunks or were torn apart in mid-limb massacres.

"Snap! There goes our pear tree, split in half. Crackle! Our giant arborvitae divided itself into thirds and took the fence. Pop! Yet another limb from a silver maple fell from about fifty feet and took the power lines—and our electricity—with it," wrote *South County Times* columnist Leslie Gibson McCarthy. It wasn't enough that the first outage came in the heat of summer, noted McCarthy. "The second one decided to arrive in the dead of autumn, thanks to an ice storm that turned the entire St. Louis area into Frozen Tundra."

For customers without power, AmerenUE recommended staying in one room, wearing layers of clothing, and wrapping in blankets. Also, the use of kerosene or charcoal heaters inside was discouraged because of carbon monoxide poisoning.

Temperatures in homes dropped to 57 degrees on Friday; Saturday, 47; Sunday, 40; Monday, 37. Cold homes sent residents to hotels, churches, city centers, and school gyms. Tree branches continued to snap; pipes started to break; patience began to disappear.

In the aftermath of the storm, power companies took it on the chin from angry mayors, the state legislature, and Missouri's Public Service Commission. One official insisted that utilities spend more time worrying about Main Street and less on catering to investors and to Wall Street.

For their part, companies resolved to invest in upkeep, stronger lines, tree trimming near power lines, and more. The Big Bad Weather Wolf was laughing and planning his next move.

In ice storms, such as the one that hit the Springfield area in 2007, rural homeowners can be without power for two weeks or longer.

During an ice storm, just a quarter inch of ice can add five hundred pounds to a power line between its supporting poles.

January 12–14, 2007; Springfield

2007: Springfield's Worst Ice Storm

t's called the North American Ice Storm of 2007. It was by far the worst such storm ever to hit the Show Me State. Folks living in Springfield don't need convincing that it was the worst winter storm ever to hit their city. The storm came in three waves out of the southwest from Friday through late Sunday, January 12–14. Ice accumulations on the I-44 corridor ranged from one to three inches and resulted in car accidents with injuries and fatalities.

Civilization came to a halt for days, because electric and telephone services were crippled by the ice storm. Utility experts note that just a quarter inch of ice adds five hundred pounds to a pole-to-pole span of power line. In the storm of 2007, linemen discovered ice as thick as soda cans on many lines.

The ice brought down trees, poles, and wires, and left residents without any electricity for weeks in many cases. Kirk Hansen, who lives in rural north Springfield, recalled three nights of giant oaks cracking, splitting, and slamming down on the icy earth. "We stood on the porch watching the ice build and talked about how much it was weighing down the tree limbs," Hansen recalled. "Then we started hearing explosions. When we followed the sounds across our horizon, we could actually see fireballs rising into the ice and clouds. We later found out that these were electric transformers exploding. Then our lights went out—kind of creepy. There was no light anywhere, only the sounds of trees breaking in the night. And it was bitterly cold."

The Hansen family home was without power for thirteen days. Phone lines succumbed to falling trees, and there were no land-line phones for a month. Hansen said it wasn't a problem since he didn't feel like talking to anyone. He turned into "kind of a grouch."

There was plenty to grouch about:

• Tree trunks blocked roads, and travel was difficult and dangerous.
• Generators were hard to find, as was the gasoline to power them.
• Long lines formed everywhere at convenience stores for basic items.
• Everything once simple was now hard: cooking, bathing, traveling.

"The QT Store brought in huge generator trailers that ran stores and gas pumps," said Hansen. "We had no water, so every day we would go to the QT simply to brush our teeth, use the restroom, and to buy coffee, the magical storm elixir." Hansen said his nearby woods are still dangerous to walk in, especially on windy days. Hundreds of trees sport broken tops, just barely hanging on, forty to one hundred feet in the air. Hansen, who handles public relations at Fantastic Caverns, said everybody pitched in for weeks to make the cave grounds safe from falling trees. "Everywhere you looked around Springfield—it was a huge mess," said Hansen. "But this wasn't just our bad experience; it was shared by almost everyone in the region."

Severe winter storms can cause aesthetic damage to parks and neighborhoods and, in exceptional cases, tangible damage that requires action by the Federal Emergency Management Agency (FEMA).

In the 2009 ice storm in the Missouri Bootheel, Ameri-Corp St. Louis sent its entire team of forty-five members to assist emergency management workers in the hardest hit areas of the region.

January 26, 2009; Sikeston and Missouri Bootheel

2009: Throwed Rolls On Ice in Sikeston

Lambert's Cafe, the famous "home of throwed rolls" in Sikeston, had been throwing muffins to customers pretty much nonstop until the ice storm of January 2009 came along. At that point, the roll-throwing came to a stop, as did pretty much everything else in southeast Missouri.

The first roll was allegedly tossed in 1976 by Norman Lambert. Norm had a habit of delivering fresh, hot rolls to tables personally. On one busy day, Norm couldn't squeeze past the crowd on his rounds, so an impatient customer yelled to just "throw the damn thing," and a tradition began. Lambert's tradition was put on hold several days after the Bootheel's most catastrophic ice storm arrived on January 26. The storm left entire towns without electricity in Kentucky, Illinois, and Missouri, including more than nine thousand customers in Sikeston.

Hundreds of wires and poles were felled by ice several inches thick from Cape Girardeau south into Arkansas. Linemen doing repairs complained of areas where ten or fifteen poles in a row were snapped and on the ground.

"I've lived in the Sikeston area all my life—thirty-seven years—and I don't ever recall anything like that ice storm," said Kelly Brown, a restaurant manager for Lambert's. "It looked like a hurricane came through for months afterward—big trees without limbs, trees and poles down everywhere."

According to Brown, Lambert's was unable to throw rolls for several days. When generators on trucks arrived, the restaurant was able to open to supply meals for repair crews that had arrived from all over the United States. "After we got power, it was still sporadic for two weeks, going on and off," said Lambert's Brown. "The Lamberts are good people, and they helped out a lot of hungry people."

The utility crews did their best to restore electricity as quickly as possible. As "quickly as possible" meant ten days and up to two weeks or more for rural homes. The storm caused eight fatalities in Missouri—some deaths by electrocution. Officials in Sikeston warned people to beware of downed wires that could still be live.

Governor Jay Nixon, who had only been in office a few days, sought help from President Barack Obama. The president declared twenty-two counties as disaster areas, and Federal Emergency Management Agency (FEMA) officials responded. The St. Louis AmeriCorp team provided shelters in nearby Doniphan, Naylor, and Poplar Bluff. "In visiting Sikeston on Thursday (January 29), I saw firsthand the destructive effects of this disaster," said Nixon. "I appreciate the president issuing this disaster declaration so Missourians will have resources to recover from this devastating storm."

At Lambert's Cafe, throwed rolls fly again, but local folks are still talking about that icy winter squall. All future ice storms will be measured up against the "Great Ice Storm of 2009."

V. HEAT WAVES AND COLD SPELLS

As this book was being readied for press in June 2009, an unusual early summer heat wave gripped St. Louis. Temperatures neared 100 degrees for more than a week, and insufferable humidity sent the heat index into triple digits. TV news began to identify the summer's first heat fatalities.

Heat waves don't offer the visual drama of a half-mile-wide marauding tornado or the sight of a farmhouse floating away in a rush of floodwater. Nevertheless, heat waves could easily be placed at the top of the charts of weather catastrophes. In a typical year, heat waves kill more people in America than all other natural disasters combined. They are quiet killers. Urban residents die behind locked doors and sealed windows. Neglected seniors bake away in hot brick homes. Workers die of heat exhaustion after failing to take the proper precautions.

Kansas City and St. Louis have endured the worst that stalled high-pressure systems and relentless sun can serve up. They may not have received the national press Chicago garnered in the deadly heat wave of 1995, but both Missouri cities have earned the unenviable reputation of having grueling spells of smothering, sultry, scorching summer sizzle.

All of this begs a few questions: Why do Kansas City and St. Louis take pride in hot, tangy, summer barbecue? Why are so many residents always outside playing or watching baseball in the heat? Why are so many homes in their urban cores made of brick? These are all mysteries to be solved in another study. What concerns us here are those long stretches of beastly heat.

Although the Show Me State was spared the worst of the 1930s' Dust Bowl, Missourians did feel the effects of merciless hot weather, severe drought, and dusty, gritty air that was unfit to breathe. Crops withered in the patchwork of fields between Kansas City and St. Louis. Columbia sweltered through a sixteen-day glut of 100-plus degree days. In the 1930s, U.S. leaders began to wonder if St. Louis was becoming the regional capital of a new, arid desert.

Terrible summer heat diminished in the 1940s, only to return with a vengeance in the early 1950s. Pat Guinan, a climatologist with the University of Missouri Extension Service, notes that 118 degrees, the highest temperature ever recorded in the state, occurred on July 14, 1954, in Union. Just up Route 66 from Union on the same day, St. Louis recorded its hottest day ever with 115 degrees.

In more recent times, St. Louisans will never forget the hot tamale heat spell of July 2006. Residents are used to powerful thunderstorms hitting the city to break a heat streak with cool relief. On July 19, 2006, a windstorm brought in a killer heat wave and knocked out the power for refrigeration and air conditioners.

The largest electrical power outage in St. Louis history, during a prolonged heat spell, necessitated the evacuation of nursing homes and centers for the elderly. National Guard troops were enlisted to help with the weather emergency. As tempers flared over the lengthy power loss, utilities like AmerenUE found themselves on the hot seat. How could a big city be without electricity for so long in such a hot spell? Long after the power was back in service, a disenchanted public and politicians continued to ask questions.

Perhaps the only thing worse than lost electricity in a hot summer is lack of power for heat in a cold winter. With its continental climate, Missouri can experience weather extremes in both seasons. Winters in the state can be mild, but they can also be notable for periods of Arctic deep freeze.

Some of the coldest winter spells ever in Missouri occurred in the first decades of the twentieth century. Cities depended on coal supplies. Residents were concerned whether city coal yards had ample reserves to fire up stoves and furnaces for the worst winter conditions. Newspaper reports kept track of the arrival of rail cars carrying coal, gas, and other fuels. Coal prices soared in the winter of 1936, when subzero temperatures hit all of the Midwest. Missouri towns like Kirksville, Columbia, Hannibal, and St. Joseph, as well as Kansas City and St. Louis, were numbed by a string of days when red mercury in the thermometer did not rise above the big goose egg—zero.

Cold in the late 1970s in the continental United States prompted some scientists to wonder whether another ice age was upon us. Some speculated about a drop in the sun's output. Solid stretches of ice in the Mississippi River in January 1977 stranded barges in St. Louis and as far south as Cairo, Illinois.

Major cold spells persisted into the winters of the early 1980s, but then the climate seemed to start warming up. By the first decade of a new century, global warming became the topic for debate among climatologists and politicians. Acknowledging the new atmospheric agenda, *Newsweek* magazine actually apologized for a cover story it ran in the 1970s about the coming ice age.

So would global warming mean more unbearable hot spells like those of the 1930s and 1950s in Missouri? According to scientists with the National Oceanic and Atmospheric Administration (NOAA), the most noticeable change for the Midwest from global warming will involve increasing humidity, storms, and flooding. Winters will be shorter and summers will be warmer.

The Dust Bowl of the 1930s in the Great Plains brought dry, dusty winds to the state of Missouri.

Highest Temperature

107 in Kansas City

Date and Location

Summer of 1930; all of Missouri

1930: Dust Bowl's Deadly Spillover

On August 3, 1930, East Coast residents moaned about the sweltering temperatures: 96 in Baltimore; 94 in Philadelphia; 92 in New York. Folks in Missouri were not impressed. Kansas City registered a blistering 107, and St. Louis notched 103. Add a dearth of rain to that tremendous heat. Intense periods of heat and a scarcity of rainfall go hand in hand, and it's not uncommon to have several weeks of blistering sun in a Missouri summer. But what if the agony stretches over many long weeks, months, even years?

The year 1930 began the decade of the Dust Bowl, which ushered in a terrible mix of heat, drought, wind, and dust storms. Although it was centered in the Great Plains, the misery in the West spilled over into Missouri.

Dust storms took tons of topsoil from the land in Nebraska, Kansas, and Oklahoma and blew much of it east across Missouri and into the states of the Ohio Valley. The citizenry of eastern Missouri wondered what they did wrong. They complained of smelling the dust and having to clean a sickly, dirty powder off their cars.

If the Dust Bowl's ill effects were a headache and an inconvenience for Missouri's urban residents, they spelled disaster for state farmers. Rows of corn simply wilted and withered. The worst drought in U.S. history reduced grain output by some hundreds of millions of bushels. Farmers in the western Missouri region looked to unrepentant skies for rain and relief in the summer of 1930. Too often they were greeted with a dry, dusty wind. If the dust looked red, it was reputed to be from Oklahoma.

Robert Geiger, an Associated Press reporter who liked sports, often gets the credit for the name "Dust Bowl," a reference to the furnace winds and all the dust afflicting the Great Plains. Geiger was familiar with the Rose Bowl and found an odd similarity in the windswept plains of Oklahoma, Kansas, and Nebraska. Missouri was on the eastern edge of Geiger's bowl.

The worst heat and dust storms came in the mid-1930s, but the grim summer of 1930 was a premonition of things to come. Agricultural experts warned the nation that a long-term catastrophe was in the making.

During the hot summer of 1930, some St. Louis residents beat the heat at night by sleeping in Forest Park or along the city's Mississippi riverfront. The strange tableau of families sprawled out on blankets in public places—long after the blazing sun retired—would be a scene repeated throughout the summers of the 1930s.

Perhaps that was the worst aspect of Missouri's Dust Bowl heat waves—the struggle to sleep when night temperatures were still in the 90s. There was no air-conditioning. There was only hope that the earth would cool down in the darkness. After a string of 100-degree days without the relief of rain, there was no such respite from the heat at night.

Divining rods have been used for centuries in an effort to find underground water, especially in times of heat and drought.

100 for 16 days

August 1936; Columbia

1936: Hot Stretch Broils Columbia

The heat, drought, dry winds, and gritty skies of the Dust Bowl years earned the 1930s a nickname: "The Dirty Thirties." In the hot summer of 1936, folks in Columbia suffered through one of the worst stretches of that cruel Dust Bowl decade. August 1936 was especially red hot. Temperatures in Missouri's premier university town soared past 100 degrees every day for a long sixteen-day stint. Columbia was at the epicenter of an intense heat wave and drought that gripped much of the country.

"This was beastly heat—and the 1930s were beastly years," explained Pat Guinan, a climatologist with the University of Missouri Extension Service. "A big part of the problem with the heat waves in 1936 and in 1934 was the Dust Bowl. These were years when the air was gritty from the dirt being swept up in the wind after months of drought.

"It was a period when the water above and below ground was at its limit," added Guinan. "The Missouri River was a trickle of itself. Wells ran dry. Farmers went out of business. It's not surprising that farmers in the Columbia area were out with divining rods looking to locate any water that might be left below the surface."

Divining rods are used in the practice of dowsing, which goes back to the ancient practice of "water witching." The idea is to take a Y-shaped branch and walk with it over the ground until it bends or twists to indicate that water may be available below the surface. Freshly cut willow or peach tree branches are used to make the rods. Skeptics dismiss divining as mere superstition. In the Middle Ages, clerics condemned its use as evidence of Satanism. In recent times, divining has been revived by those involved in nature religions, witchcraft, or Wicca.

In 1936, it's doubtful the Columbia farmers were interested in ancient superstitions or witchcraft. They were out in the heat with their handcrafted water witches because they were desperate to find water. Farmers were also cutting tree branches to feed the livestock. Pastures were parched. Agricultural losses were enormous in 1936. Crops were a total loss in some areas, where soils lost their fertility due to extreme heat. The dry, exposed, and dead soil acted like desert terrain, radiating rather than absorbing the heat of the sun.

The U.S. death toll in the 1936 heat wave reached five thousand. Many of those fatalities occurred in metropolises like Kansas City and St. Louis. Urban areas became giant ovens in 1936.

"Nobody gets used to day after day of 100-plus degrees. What was worse were all those nights when there was no cool down and no air-conditioning," said Guinan of Columbia. "We haven't seen exceptionally hot stretches like the 1930s or 1950s for decades, but I am a firm believer that if we had them in the past, we can have them again."

Horses need access to plenty of water when temperatures soar above 100, but in 1952 horses in the city of St. Louis were revived with half pints of rum.

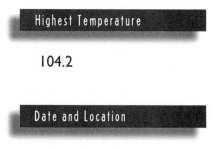

Highest Temperature

104.2

Date and Location

June 1952; St. Louis

1952: Too Hot for Fowl, Horse, and Human

The Weatherbird on the front page of the *St. Louis Post-Dispatch* was warm, winded, and fanning itself profusely. "Turn it off, Mr. Weatherman!" was the captioned cry of the famous fowl, as sweat flew from its fevered brow.

On June 25, 1952, the poor old Weatherbird could not have known that this was just the beginning of one of the hottest summers on record. Temperatures catapulted from the 90s and into the 100s by month's end.

Little relief came with July and August. Some heat records were tied. Others were broken. The weather was not fit for the *Post*'s illustrious fowl, for man, or for beast. The beasts that took a particular beating from the brutal beams of a blowtorch sun were those of an equestrian nature. For horses, it was simply too hot to trot. On June 29, the *Post* sported a front-page head about seven horses in the city succumbing to exhaustion by heat. However, it noted that six of the horses were revived by rum.

"This is the worst summer on horses I have ever seen," Sergeant Lee Potter of the Humane Society told the *Post-Dispatch*. "We are taking drastic measures. Every time we see a horse on the street, we order the driver to rest the animal for a half hour."

In the case of the seven horses that collapsed downtown, six were given a half pint of rum each. The administered sugarcane spirits revived the flagging spirits of the horses. The rum reportedly restored their circulation. The seventh horse succumbed to the St. Louis summer apocalypse.

Vets who work for the Humane Society today say they would refrain from any equine rum fix. They argue that a spike in the heat doesn't really signal the need for a rum-spiked drink for a dehydrated horse.

"I think rum may be an outdated procedure—not something we would do now," said Dawn Mrad, a vet with Mid-Rivers Equine Centre, who also works for the Humane Society. "Horses do like the taste of alcohol, but it's doubtful a half pint would have much effect on such big animals.

"Horses were probably at the end of the line for use by haulers in downtown St. Louis by the early 1950s," added Mrad. "Horses can be grateful now that most owners are much more cautious about their health today."

The 1952 *Post* story on downtown's overheated horses was overshadowed by a lead story on the heat's human cost. June 29, the hottest day in sixteen years in St. Louis, had taken another toll: eight human lives. The 104.2 temperature buckled city streets; reduced tar roadways to goo; and strained supplies of water and electricity, as residents used both for different methods of cooling down.

Out in the tiny St. Louis suburb of Kirkwood, officials told residents to chill it on sprinkling their lawns and hot children. They also told them to cool it on around-the-clock use of fans. That use was causing power outages.

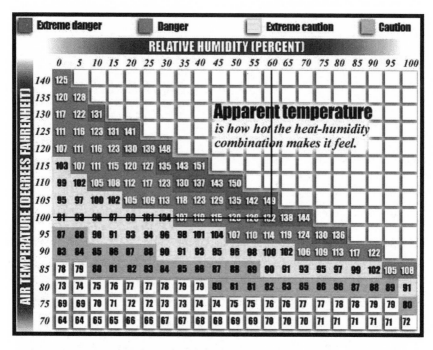

The summer of 1954 was hot enough even without the so-called "heat index," which factors in the effect of humidity in combination with rising temperatures.

Highest Temperature

115 in St. Louis; 118 in St. Louis, Warsaw, and Union

Date and Location

July 14, 1954; St. Louis, Warsaw, and Union

1954: The Hottest Day Ever in St. Louis

Years before there were formulas for "sultriness" and a calculation for a heat index, hot summer days came upon the state of Missouri. In fact, the official hottest day ever recorded in St. Louis was July 14, 1954, when the mercury topped out at 115 degrees.

Several locations beat St. Louis on that day for the "Show Me Hot Spot." Just down the road from the Gateway City, the town of Union hit 118 degrees, as did the town of Warsaw in Ozark country. According to Pat Guinan, a climatologist with the University of Missouri Extension Service, 118 is the highest temperature recorded in the state.

Of course, a lot more people were affected by the 115 in St. Louis than the 118 in Union or in Warsaw. The newspapers in St. Louis were filled with columns about the effects of the scorching heat, as well as the names of unfortunate residents who expired in the incredibly hot weather. "Hopefully, we won't have a repeat of that kind of heat any time soon in St. Louis," said James Kramper of the National Weather Service office for St. Louis. "That kind of heat puts a lot of people at risk, especially the elderly and the young."

Would it have felt much hotter in St. Louis in 1954 if weather forecasters had been talking about the heat index for that terrible day? Perhaps from a psychological point it would have felt even more miserable.

Fortunately, R. G. Steadman had not come along yet to invent the heat index. This neat invention would not arrive until the late 1970s. Steadman came up with a complex formula to determine how a fictional person might feel hotter if humidity was factored in with excessive temperatures. Steadman's formula was simplified by the Weather Service. An example of this formula might be a 90-degree day with a 65 percent humidity pushing the heat index to over 100. The heat index indicates that you feel like it's more than 100 degrees outside, even though it's actually 90. It's all about humidity.

Humidity is said to intensify the effects of a heat wave. Moist air just feels hotter than dry air. On a hot and dry day, sweat evaporates faster on skin and cools the body down. The natural cooling system tends to go on the fritz when the humidity is high and pushes up the heat index.

"If we had the relative humidity for July 14, 1954, we could figure out the heat index," said St. Louis meteorologist Kramper. "But I am willing to wager that the humidity was really low that day. When it gets up to 115 degrees, that usually only can happen when it's a very dry day. It's like the heat that you find in America's Southwest.

"If the global climate change forecasts are correct, it may be a long time before we see 115 again in Missouri," added Kramper. "If global climate change brings more precipitation, downpours, and flooding for us in the Midwest, we won't get the dry heat that gives us 115 temperatures."

When stationary high-pressure systems bring record summer heat to the Midwest, it's time to drag out the sprinklers for the kids.

Highest Temperature

100 for 15 days

Date and Location

Summer of 1980; Kansas City

1980: Kansas City's Summer Simmer

xperts in meteorology have honed in on the great 1980 Heat Wave that toasted all of Missouri. Their scientific studies deconstruct the protracted heat and intense drought of one of the most scorching summers ever. Jerome Namias of the University of California outlines the effects of an upper-level continental high-pressure system with associated subsidence, dry soil, lack of clouds, and high insolation. All of this resulted in an unrelenting heat, according to Namias.

Thomas R. Karl and Robert G. Quayle of the National Climatic Data Center in Asheville, North Carolina, attribute the oppressive weather to a northerly migration of the westerlies. The loss of the storm-carrying westerlies, combined with a stationary anticyclone of high pressure, led to a pronounced drying and heating of the air.

Kansas City folks who endured the summer of 1980 won't tell you about anticyclones, declines in potential evapotranspiration, or an alarming soil moisture abnormality index. They will tell you it was damned hot and too darned dry for a solitary blade of grass—and even most weeds.

Heat in 1980 was tough on cities from New Mexico to South Carolina, but Missouri was roasted on red coals. Kansas City was spiked on the bottom spit of a national barbecue pit. Cow Town thermometers soared above 100 for more than fifteen days straight. The low temps barely slipped below 90.

This was no laughing matter. The "frying eggs on asphalt" jokes simply evaporated by the end of July. This summer was deadly, costly, and on a par with the traumatic heat waves of 1930–36 and 1952–54. The inner-city Kansas City area—with its blacktop, concrete, and brick—became an incendiary incubator of death that July. Local television news was peppered with reports of heat cramps, heat exhaustion, heat strokes, and all manner of heat-related deaths.

Mortality rates in the suffocating 1980 heat disaster prompted anger and disturbing questions. How many deaths were directly attributed to the torrid weather? What could have been done to prevent the fatalities? What might city safety officials do to prepare for future heat emergencies?

Weather experts had questions to ponder as well. Why did conventional long-range forecasts fail to predict the record-breaking conditions? Why did conditions in the Pacific Ocean affect weather in Kansas City? How were unusually cold surface temperatures in parts of the Pacific responsible for the layer-cake levels of heat over the entire state of Missouri?

Of course, Missouri was just one big piece of a continental calamity. The economic hit on the United States was close to $20 billion (twice that in today's dollars) due to livestock and crop losses, infrastructure damage, and energy costs. Nationwide, more than 1,250 deaths were tied directly to 1980's extreme heat.

Children enjoy water fun in the worst of summer's heat waves, while the National Guard delivers bottled water to residents sweltering in homes without power.

Highest Temperature

115 heat indices

Date and Location

July 2006; St. Louis

2006: Sweating It Out in St. Louis

July 2006 will long be remembered in the St. Louis area. Air-conditioning seemed a necessity as temperatures each afternoon topped out around the century mark. And then, the strange storm of July 19 blew into the region from an unlikely direction via Illinois.

Thousands of people got the fright of their lives at a Cardinals game in Busch Stadium when eighty mile-per-hour winds slammed the downtown. Fans began taking cover wherever they could and wondered whether the flying debris was the prelude to a tornado hit. Brick walls, radio towers, and roofs collapsed as the storm moved from the riverfront into St. Louis County. Trees ripped from their roots and crashing limbs took out power lines leaving 500,000 without electricity.

A second storm two days later reversed the progress utility crews were making in restoring power. Several hundred thousand more customers were left without electricity. Even worse—the Heat Wave of 2006 persisted with high humidity and heat indices up to 115 degrees.

Electric generators disappeared from box store retailers. Grocery stores shipped in thousands of bags of ice from nearby states to keep up with demand. Emergency personnel and paramedics tried to respond to all the calls from chronically ill people. Many depended on home electrical health devices to keep them alive.

Several days into the crisis, the National Guard was called out. The soldiers did storm cleanup and went door-to-door in areas where the elderly were trying to survive the heat.

Under siege from public officials and unhappy consumers, the utility AmerenUE issued a plea for patience, noting that the damage to its energy delivery system was the worst in one hundred years of service. The company said it was being overwhelmed by as many as forty thousand calls per hour.

Leah Merriman, a future journalist and college newspaper editor in St. Louis, monitored the situation in total awe. She was even more amazed, however, when her aunt from Florida called. Merriman thought her aunt was checking to see if she made it through the storms, power outages, and unbelievable heat wave. Merriman's aunt said she heard on the news that about 174,000 residents were without power in New York City, but nothing about a disaster in St. Louis. "For having such extreme weather conditions—such as snow at the end of April and wearing shorts at Christmas—St. Louis sure gets snubbed," wrote Merriman in a piece for her college paper in August.

"When it comes to danger, however, that's supposedly our city's middle name. St. Louis gets ranked as the most dangerous city," she continued. "Yet, it did not have a single incident of looting reported during the weeks without electricity. That's more than can be said for the twenty-five-hour blackout in New York City in 1977. . . ."

Ice gorges form in narrow stretches of river and can bring boat traffic to a complete stop.

-18

February 13, 1905; St. Louis

1905: When River Ice Gorges Terrorized

A century ago, a major category in the catalog of natural disasters faced by river towns was the ice gorge. With today's milder winters, waterways regulated by locks and dams, and sturdier river vessels, we don't hear as much about ice gorges and their threat to life and property.

In an earlier American epoch, ice gorges snarled river traffic and terrorized river towns. Waterways would first freeze due to an extended cold spell, then a sudden thaw would break up large chunks of ice. Great ice gorges would bubble up, slam into tugs and barges, pile up in natural dams, and beach themselves on shorelines to cause all kinds of damage. Stories about frightful ice jams on the Missouri and Mississippi rivers were regular fare in the St. Louis–based *Waterways Journal* during cold decades of the early twentieth century. The rivers froze over completely in those years, and residents crossed "ice bridges" without paying tolls.

In January and February 1905, consecutive days of below-zero weather piled up like ice on the river. The Mississippi closed south to Cape Girardeau and beyond. Attempts by boat fleets to keep the St. Louis harbor open resulted in heavily damaged and grounded ships. Thick ice floes formed a dam, and river levels dropped dangerously. Boats seeking to forge through the dark ice gorge were holed, stoved, or buckled, which usually resulted in sinking.

Mariners could always count on treacherous navigation problems in the ice-forming season. Sometimes the ice was dynamited for relief. "In the old days, ice gorges were a problem," explained Nelson "Spence" Spencer of the *Waterways Journal* in a 2009 interview. "Today, ice can still accumulate above the locks and can cause problems. The last time ice gorges caused problems for St. Louis shipping was in the late 1970s."

Alan Dooley, public affairs officer for the Army Corps of Engineers, said that in the years before locks and dams, extreme cold meant extreme problems on the Mississippi and Missouri rivers. An ice gorge would form in a narrow part of the river and literally dam up the water. When it all broke loose, all hell broke loose—a tsunami rushed downstream. Sometimes an ice gorge would break up and crunch and crash with primordial screeching. Sounds like cannon or pistol shots would emanate from the vicinity of battling ice monsters banging heads in the river.

Up from the levee, the citizenry of St. Louis in 1905 was less concerned with the ice on the river than the ice under their frozen feet and the ice under their carriage horses. Newspapers in St. Louis in the bitter winter of 1905 were filled with accounts of broken arms and legs as well as deadly concussions. The trials and tribulations of boatmen were a mere trifle compared to the woes of the city's many fallen pedestrians.

Wind (mph)	Temperature (°F)																	
Calm	40	35	30	25	20	15	10	5	0	-5	-10	-15	-20	-25	-30	-35	-40	-45
5	36	31	25	19	13	7	1	-5	-11	-16	-22	-28	-34	-40	-46	-52	-57	-63
10	34	27	21	15	9	3	-4	-10	-16	-22	-28	-35	-41	-47	-53	-59	-66	-72
15	32	25	19	13	6	0	-7	-13	-19	-26	-32	-39	-45	-51	-58	-64	-71	-77
20	30	24	17	11	4	-2	-9	-15	-22	-29	-35	-42	-48	-55	-61	-68	-74	-81
25	29	23	16	9	3	-4	-11	-17	-24	-31	-37	-44	-51	-58	-64	-71	-78	-84
30	28	22	15	8	1	-5	-12	-19	-26	-33	-39	-46	-53	-60	-67	-73	-80	-87
35	28	21	14	7	0	-7	-14	-21	-27	-34	-41	-48	-55	-62	-69	-76	-82	-89
40	27	20	13	6	-1	-8	-15	-22	-29	-36	-43	-50	-57	-64	-71	-78	-84	-91
45	26	19	12	5	-2	-9	-16	-23	-30	-37	-44	-51	-58	-65	-72	-79	-86	-93
50	26	19	12	4	-3	-10	-17	-24	-31	-38	-45	-52	-60	-67	-74	-81	-88	-95
55	25	18	11	4	-3	-11	-18	-25	-32	-39	-46	-54	-61	-68	-75	-82	-89	-97
60	25	17	10	3	-4	-11	-19	-26	-33	-40	-48	-55	-62	-69	-76	-84	-91	-98

Frostbite Times ▢ 30 minutes ▢ 10 minutes ▢ 5 minutes

$$Wind\ Chill\ (°F) = 35.74 + 0.6215T - 35.75(V^{0.16}) + 0.4275T(V^{0.16})$$

Where, T= Air Temperature (°F) V= Wind Speed (mph)

Effective 11/01/01

Wind chill factors were not widely used until the late 1970s, but it felt cold enough without such calculations in the winter of 1917.

Lowest Temperature

-18

Date and Location

January 1917; St. Louis

1917: Sensationalizing Winter's Chill

On an unusually cold day in the fall of 1865, an ambitious immigrant named Joseph Pulitzer reached the banks of the Mississippi River. The future newspaper mogul shivered in the chill, but he sought out a ferry operator to get him across the river. "The lights of St. Louis looked like a promised land to me," recalled the young Pulitzer.

He went on to found a new kind of journalism—exciting and sensational—put to the test in his *St. Louis Post-Dispatch*. According to biographer W. A. Swanberg, Pulitzer brought news to life. He sensationalized political chicanery, crime, corruption—even bad weather. Years after his death in 1911, editors and reporters continued the style he perfected for making the news vital and important for average folks.

The Pulitzer imprint was evident in the way his *Post-Dispatch* covered the cruel winter of 1917. Papers were filled with dark headlines and a series of strident heads and copy that would make you think Siberia had migrated to St. Louis along with Pulitzer. A January 1917 edition screamed out: "Storm Virtually Isolates the City; No Relief Today." More headliness continued: "Railroads Offer No Hope That Passenger Service Will Be Restored Tonight at Earliest—Many Travelers Stranded." Still more headlines on the same story told of winter's treachery: "Snow Drifted by Wind Which at Times Yesterday Reached Velocity of 40 Miles—Interurban Line Shut Down; Lowest Point Reached by Mercury 17 Degrees Below Zero, Coldest Here in Nearly 13 Years."

Editors made darn sure everyone knew about unprecedented cold in 1917. It described motorists driving across the frozen Missouri River at St. Charles. It noted that the city at -18 was only five degrees away from the coldest temperature ever recorded in St. Louis: Twenty-three below zero on January 29, 1873. In one 1917 edition, the *Post* found comfort in a day when the winds were quiet: "This morning's cold was of the still, Northern sort, and was not accompanied by the blizzardy, prairie-like winds which [make] outdoor life almost unbearable. . . ."

In other 1917 editions, the paper blamed the cold air on Canada, saying it originated in north Saskatchewan. The paper took some cruel delight in describing snow-laden gales blowing harshly off the tundra-like prairie.

Imagine what these papers might have done with today's reports on wind chill factors! Wind chill was not widely used until the 1970s. The controversial index combines cold and wind to provide a reading as to how the chill feels on exposed skin surface, due to winter gales and gusts. On a cold January 13, 1917, the *Post-Dispatch* could have reported wind chills down to 55 below zero due to the howling winds. It's doubtful such extreme reporting would have inspired any heated arguments from readers.

Extreme cold can result in huge fruit crop losses in the Missouri–Illinois region with a corresponding hike in prices for foodstuffs.

Lowest Temperature

20 days of below 0

Date and Location

Winter 1936

1936: Subzero Misery Zaps Missouri

"All of the state of Missouri experiences 'extreme' climate events, and such events must be considered part of the normal climate," declares the Missouri Climate Center at the University of Missouri in Columbia. If extremes are normal in the Show Me State, then 1936 has to rank as the most normal year in Missouri weather history. The state suffered a record heat wave in the summer of 1936 after it endured a record cold wave in the frigid winter of that year.

The summer heat was just part of "The Dirty Thirties" Dust Bowl decade, an endless epoch of drought and unwelcome strings of cruel 100-plus degree days. Federal officials came to fret that St. Louis was becoming the capital of a vast inland desert being created in the United States.

So, what was the deal with the extremely cold winter of 1936? How could such a cold year punctuate a period of oven-baked cities and parched rural pastures in Missouri? Blame it on the continental climate characterized by "strong seasonality." Cold air masses, unimpeded by any topographical barriers, swooped down from Canada and put Missouri in the deep freeze.

The extreme cold fronts may not have been totally abnormal for Missouri, but life's normal routines were brought to a standstill. St. Louis went for twenty days straight with no above-zero temperature readings. Businesses shuttered. Schools closed. Residents shivered in homes with frozen water pipes and without a constant supply of electricity. Fire departments answered frantic calls involving homes set ablaze by overheated stoves and furnaces.

Forget all that postal service mythology—the lyrical legends about how "neither snow nor rain, nor heat nor gloom of night" keep the mail couriers from the swift completion of their appointed rounds. Mail service was interrupted for days by the cold of 1936.

Coal prices soared in the winter of 1936, as did the prices for earmuffs, scarves, gloves, and mittens. Prices for foodstuffs also rocketed, and the prospects for fruit crops in the spring were wiped out. Mercury thermometers were rendered useless. The so-called "layered look" for the outdoors encompassed three, four, and five coatings of clothing—even more for water department workers.

The winter season of 1936 was not just tough on Missouri. According to the Associated Press, wind chills in the Dakotas approached 100 degrees below zero. A 56 degrees below zero reading was recorded in International Falls, Minnesota. Many rivers froze solid in Missouri and Illinois. Wildlife losses from the cold were unprecedented in many rural locations. The wildlife on the front page of the *St. Louis Post-Dispatch* also was affected by the calamitous cold. The newspaper's bundled-up Weatherbird plaintively declared: "Can't we find a sub for sub-zero?"

Winter snowmen seem to be oblivious to any theories about global cooling or global warming.

Lowest Temperature

-12

Date and Location

January 17, 1977; St. Louis

1977: Missouri's Year of Global Cooling

In the cold, snowy January of 1977, Missourians kept their scarves and earmuffs handy for days. Ice packs and ice gorges were forming on the sluggish Mississippi and Missouri rivers—not that anybody was very interested in taking a winter swim. What folks were interested in was: Why did it seem like this cold wave was in Missouri for an entire season, not just for a spell? Where was the "January Thaw" that Missourians always counted on to help them get through winter's worst?

Scientists offered more than one theory to explain the unprecedented cold wave. Perhaps that's because all over the United States, the weather experts were confined to the great indoors by the cold. They had time on their hands for plenty of theorizing.

Planetary Scale Forcing was one incredible explanation for the 1977 cold wave. According to J. P. McGuirk, a scholar in atmospheric sciences at Colorado State University, typical weather patterns in the northern hemisphere had turned atypical. McGurk's hypothesis was that high pressure "blocking ridges" developed over the oceans with the result that the North Pole warmed, the mid-latitudes cooled, and the continental temperatures plunged. Such abnormal phenomena had occurred in 1958 and 1963 as well. Other explanations were offered to account for the succession of minus-degree days in St. Louis and the Midwest.

These hypotheses focused on the shifting of deep ocean currents, which act as conveyors of climate change. Ocean surface temperatures associated with El Niño and La Niña also entered the picture.

A third explanation for the severe cold suggested a global cooling and the possibility that a new ice age was commencing. In this scenario, man's agricultural and industrial pollution was bringing down temperatures and ushering in a new glacial age. Indeed, two years before the glacial cold of 1977 hit Missouri, *Newsweek* magazine noted the onset of a "minor ice age" beginning in 1945. *Newsweek* chided government leaders for not taking such actions as stockpiling food. Noting a half-degree drop in average temperatures from 1945 to 1968, *Newsweek* stated that "the present decline has taken the planet about a sixth of the way toward the Ice Age."

Many climate scientists expressed skepticism over the 1975 cover story. They were, at best, uncertain about the future. Three decades after its ice age prediction appeared, *Newsweek* issued a rather late correction, declaring the story's assertions about an ice age to be "spectacularly wrong."

One thing is for sure, in old, cold St. Louis, no one in 1977 was talking about any global warming. Frozen pipes broke. Cars wouldn't start. Snow wouldn't melt. Records for cold were being set. The awful global cooling was a more likely conversation.

An Amur tiger cub enjoys the results of a snowfall at the Saint Louis Zoo. Lions and tigers cope with cold and snow better than most humans.

Lowest Temperature

-2

Date and Location

February 1, 1982; St. Louis

1982: Winter's Happening at the Zoo

I f you happen to be a human, you are basically a tropical animal, which means you are a wimp when it comes to cold spells. Even mild cold makes you uncomfortable, making your teeth chatter and your body shiver. Chills run down your spine. Fortunately, humans who came before you found ways to counter the cold. They passed on their tricks to succeeding generations. Their two major solutions to dealing with outdoor cold: Consume food high in carbohydrate content, and wear clothing that keeps out nasty moisture and wickedly frigid winds.

In the cold and snowy January of 1982, Missourians relied heavily on these two pivotal solutions to the cold. In St. Louis, where cars were stalled and streets were impassable, most residents who ventured outdoors chose to rely on the two proven cold-coping mechanisms.

Many could not travel to the major grocery chains, so they walked in the snow to convenience stores to stock up on hot dogs, milk, candy bars, and hot chocolate. On those walks, they wore boots, gloves, flannel shirts, oversized sweaters, and coats with hoods.

Humans have learned to cope with cold from the north, but what about the zoo animals? What precautions can they take when snow piles up and winter winds blow? Actually, they're pretty much at the mercy of their human keepers. At the Saint Louis Zoo, reptiles and amphibians are sensitive to the cold, but so are primates and other species of tropical animals. In the harsh winter of 1982, they depended on Steve Bircher, a zoo manager who is now curator of mammals.

"The 1982 winter season is one that I will always remember," said Bircher. "I was commissary supervisor for the animals. It was not only cold, but we had one of the worst snowstorms in a decade. I was one of the few people with four-wheel drive at the time, and I used it to go from animal house to animal house to get them fed."

Another concern was the electric heaters in use in the reptile and amphibian areas. These became critical. Emergency power generators were on hand for electricity interruptions from downed power lines.

Surprisingly, lions and tigers cope with cold and snow better than most humans. Although they don't have much tolerance for blowing snow and blizzard-like conditions, they will play in the snow and will find their favorite exposed rock for some lounging.

The Saint Louis Zoo kept its animals comfortable and well adjusted in the stormy winter of 1982. Bircher said, at times, it was a challenge. "We just haven't had a winter that brutal since," Bircher said. "I can't say it's because of global warming for sure, but all the carbon dioxide we are adding to the atmosphere can't be good. We should err on the side of caution and reduce these pollutants."

POSTSCRIPT: Whither the Weather?

Why in the name of Dorothy and Toto are supercell tornado outbreaks happening in the winter in Missouri? Tornado season is supposed to begin in April, but in January of 2008, tornadoes fell out of Missouri skies by the dozens. What's up with that?

Snowstorms used to be the big winter story in Missouri, but now it's all about ice storms. They knocked out power in the Missouri Bootheel in 2009, Springfield in 2007, St. Louis in 2006. Killer ice storms are hitting every winter. What's up with that?

As for torrential rains and rivers out of their banks, it used to be that those five hundred-year floods would come a couple of times a millennium. Now it seems like the flood of the century is happening every other year—2008 was the wettest year on record in St. Louis. What's up with that?

And why are these nine-banded armadillos thriving in Missouri? They are supposed to be happier in the Texas heat. Now, these hard-shelled creatures seem to be on their way to Canada in a migration through the Show Me State. Armadillo road kill is everywhere in the state. What's up with that?

There's plenty of agreement in Missouri that the first decade of the new century has witnessed strange weather events and a bit of climate change. However, opinion is divided among both average residents and meteorologists in local media as to whether continuing climate change is being brought on by what scientists call "global warming."

Hundreds of world scientists with the Intergovernmental Panel on Climate Change do believe that global warming is a fact and affecting weather in the United States. In 2009, scientists noted that eight of the past ten years were among the warmest on record. Of course, global warming doesn't necessarily mean that Missouri will become as hot and dry as the Desert Southwest, according to scientists who are certain it is occurring. Some locales will become much warmer and others will become colder as a result of changes in the ocean currents.

As this book was readied for press, the White House released the report *Global Climate Change Impacts in the United States*. According to the report, Missouri and the Midwest will experience heavier downpours and increased flooding in the years ahead because of global warming. Specifically, precipitation is projected to increase in winter and spring and to become more intense throughout the year. The pattern is expected to lead to more frequent flooding, increasing infrastructure damage, and detrimental impacts on human health. The Midwest has experienced two record-breaking floods in the past score of years. Heavy downpours are now twice as frequent as they were a century ago, and flooding rains are projected to increase further in Missouri as regions of the globe continue to warm.

Despite all the alarm, many of the Missouri TV meteorologists, who helped with advice and information for this study, remain skeptical. They resist any suggestions that climate change and global warming should become part of the content of their daily weather reports. Other weather forecasters in Missouri, surveyed for this book, are more sympathetic to the idea. They think it's appropriate to occasionally cover global warming and its effects as part of daily weather fare for local audiences—and they have done just that. "I did a global warming special for our station on the 10 p.m. newscast," said Gary Lezak, chief meteorologist with KSHB-TV in Kansas City. "Overall, I am uncertain that in a ten-year period we will notice much in a trend. Every year is different when it comes to weather."

According to Kent Ehrhardt, meteorologist with KMOV-TV in St. Louis, the state of Missouri has to rank in the top ten of unpredictable weather war zones in the country—and global warming just makes the climate all that more interesting. Ehrhardt said the St. Louis station has mentioned global warming's impact in forecasts. "I expect more extreme weather on a global scale as a result of growing climate change," Ehrhardt said. He added that those armadillos tracking through Missouri are evidence of the warming climate in the state.

Dave Snider with KY3-TV, the local NBC affiliate in Springfield, Missouri, is one Show Me State meteorologist who has no problem mentioning the issue of global warming on TV—or during his forays into the local community. "We're battling the talk radio show nonsense, and the anti–climate change propaganda in some local churches, that can be simply overwhelming," said Snider. "If you mention climate change or global warming, snickers erupt and smirks draw over faces in the room. Moreover, the local effects seem hard to quantify anyway. That makes it very difficult to show viewers, 'here is climate change in the Ozarks.'"

Nevertheless, Snider said it is possible to point to more variability in weather patterns in the Ozarks and to changes in habitat, which serve as signs that global warming is, indeed, having some obvious effect in southern Missouri. "I try to find simple things to point to," said Snider, "The increase in armadillos, road runners, and the scissor-tailed flycatcher. All are moving north as their habitat moves northward. And magnolia trees seem more hearty in southern Missouri than I ever remember as a child."

Hundreds of scientists at the 2009 world climate change conference in Copenhagen insisted that evidence for global warming is irrefutable in the melting glaciers, loss of ice sheets, and increase in sea levels. Some of those climate scientists argue that meteorologists, who often are the only reporters on TV with science backgrounds, should sound the alarm as part of their responsibility to their audiences. Despite the scientists' assertions, there is some hesitation in Missouri to wade into the global warming controversy. Reluctance to explain the impact of global warming on weather in television newscasts seems more pronounced in Missouri than some other states. That may be so because many Missourians, who embrace anti-environmentalist talk show pundits like Rush Limbaugh as one of their own, scoff at the idea of climate change as an effect of modern-day carbon emissions.

Eric Aldrich, a meteorologist at KOMU-TV, the NBC affiliate in Columbia associated with the University of Missouri School of Journalism, doesn't see a need to get into the climate shift subject on broadcasts. Aldrich believes there is not enough time to mention global warming on TV weather segments and that it is too controversial a topic. "Global warming is a climate issue and is not related to the weather per se," said Aldrich. "It really has no place in a local weathercast."

Longtime St. Louis weatherman Dave Murray of KTVI-TV, FOX2, said he prefers to talk about climate change and weather cycles over global warming. Murray said, "The climate is always changing and has been since day one" and will continue to do so. "We have been in a warmer than average pattern for the last ten to fifteen years," said Murray. "That cycle is now just starting to flip to a colder than average pattern that will last fifteen to twenty years, although there will be some blips in this pattern."

Cindy Preszler, chief meteorologist for KSDK-TV, NewsChannel 5 in St. Louis, said she thinks it is, in fact, appropriate to mention global warming and its impact on weather in TV forecasts. She said the station has occasionally done just that. "I believe our weather will become more drastic . . . hotter and drier," said Preszler. "There will be more severe weather. As the planet warms, it affects the atmosphere."

John Fuller, a St. Louis meteorologist formerly with KSDK who now forecasts for KPLR-TV, Channel 11, said he has no hesitancy to mention global warming in the right context in broadcasts. He is a believer in the earth's warming and its impact on global and local weather. "I expect more extremes in all weather due to global warming," said Fuller. "More heat energy means more lift in the atmosphere, which means more thunderstorms and tornadoes as a result, along with more heavy rain events and winter storms."

Bryan Busby, who got his start in TV weather forecasting at KTVI in St. Louis, now is chief meteorologist for KMBC-TV in Kansas City, the ABC affiliate. Busby said he doesn't think global warming is useful to mention in local weather forecasting. "No way, I think global warming can't be quantified on a daily basis," said Busby. "It is a trend of change taking place over many, many years."

The debate over whether to bring the global warming issue into the local weather was put at the top of the agenda in 2007. That's when noted meteorologist Heidi Cullen of the Weather Channel argued that TV forecasters should be more than willing to make the link between weather changes and the global warming caused by greenhouse gas emissions. Cullen went a step further on her Internet blog and suggested that any forecasters who publicly questioned global warming as a man-made problem should have their own professional certifications called into question. She said skeptics of man's role in pushing up the planet's temperatures ought to have their American Meteorological Society (AMS) seals of approval revoked.

The comments by the Weather Channel's Cullen inspired a predictable backlash. The Drudge Report and texters in the blogosphere accused Cullen of scare tactics and of intolerance toward other viewpoints. John Coleman, who is no longer with the Weather Channel but who founded it, dismissed the idea of man-made global warming as simply "a scam." He said the idea was contrived by greedy scientists in search of grants and environmentalists with ulterior political motives.

"Even that lady on the Weather Channel probably gets paid good money for a prime time show on climate change. No man-made global warming—no show, and no salary," were the comments of an unhappy meteorologist on the *National Review* magazine's Online Media Blog. "The climate of this planet has been changing since God put the planet here," the meteorologist continued. "It will always change, and the warming of the last ten years is not much different than the warming we saw in the 1930s and other decades."

Back in Missouri, TV weather forecasters complain that there simply isn't enough time to explore global warming's causes and consequences on the average television weather report in the 6 p.m. or 10 p.m. newscast slots. "I have no more than three minutes, with less than one minute of discretionary time in my broadcasts," said Bob Reeves of KFVS-TV, Channel 12, in Cape Girardeau. Reeves said there also is not enough data on the impact of global warming on local weather to include it in a broadcast. Lisa Teachman of KMBC-TV in Kansas City agrees with Reeves. She said the topic is too controversial. Also, when it comes to the notion that global warming is having an impact on weather, there is "not enough data to prove it."

Zach Paul, weather forecaster for KRCG-TV in Jefferson City, said Missouri weather is always topsy-turvy with spring temperatures in the winter and cold spells in the spring. He indicated global warming would be too controversial for inclusion in his weather broadcasts.

"To say Missouri will get affected by this [global warming's impact] is impossible," said Jeff Penner of KSHB-TV in Kansas City. "I think global warming may be showing some effect. We are noticing bigger and more frequent rain events." Penner said the station has had a special on global warming, "but it does not have much place in a regular weather broadcast."

Gary Bandy of KSNF-TV in Joplin said he has talked about global warming and its impact on weather while doing his job as a forecaster. He said audiences are skeptical. "Southwest Missouri is the most conservative corner of one of the most conservative states in the country, and you would have a hard time finding more people who steadfastly refuse to believe in climate change than right here in this area." Bandy said. "As I've mentioned a time or two when speaking to the public regarding weather in the area, partisanship has gone out of control when something as nerdy as climatology is regarded as a hot-button political issue."

There are very few actual meteorologists or climatologists or scientists these days who deny the facts of the matter," Bandy added. "You'll hear politicians and pundits piping up against it but when you actually look at the science of the issue, there's not much evidence there to dispute the fact that the climate has changed. "As I've explained it to my son, it all boils down to simple math . . . if you pump out 100 parts of particulate aerosols into the atmosphere, those 100 parts will affect the atmosphere in one way or another. If you pee in clear water, it becomes yellow. Seems pretty simple to me."

Another thing that's pretty obvious to anyone who has lived in Missouri is the "intriguing changeability" of the state's weather. No less an observer than writer Mark Twain has had plenty to say about the weather battles which take place in the heavens above Missouri. As emphasized in the preface to this book, Missouri has many long spells of fine weather. Its winters can be mild; its springs can be inspiring; its sunny summers can make the state an incredible playground; its autumns are incomparably awesome. Nevertheless, Missouri has more than its share of heat and drought, ice and snow, straight winds and tornadoes, cloudbursts and flooding. The state's meteorological history is mind-boggling in its intensity and diversity. And there's more to come. So stand by, please—plenty of tales of nature's wrath in Missouri are yet to unfold and yet to be told.

FUJITA TORNADO SCALE

The Fujita Tornado Scale, usually referred to as the F-Scale, classifies tornadoes based on the resulting damage. This scale was developed by Dr. T. Theodore Fujita (University of Chicago) in 1971.

F-SCALE	WINDS	TYPE OF DAMAGE
F0	40-72 mph	Slight Damage: Some damage to chimneys and roofs, antennas, branches broken off, trees bent, and signs pushed over.
F1	73-112 mph	Moderate Damage: Carports destroyed, weakened trees uprooted, mobile homes sustain damage, noticeable property loss.
F2	113-157 mph	Major Damage: Roofs blown off homes, trees snapped and fences crushed, sheds demolished, and mobile homes overturned.
F3	158-206 mph	Severe Damage: Outside walls and roofs blown off homes. Buildings prone to collapse or complete destruction. Trees and crops flattened.
F4	207-260 mph	Devastating Damage: Well-built homes demolished. Large steel and concrete construction thrown for distances with sometimes deadly consequences.
F5	261-318 mph	Incredible Tornadic Damage: Homes and autos take flight, disappear. Schools, motels, and other larger structures crushed with walls and roofs lost. Rare phenomenon, but not unprecedented.

Record Temperatures

Top 10 Hottest Days

	St. Louis	Columbia	Springfield
1	115° F - July 14, 1954	113° F - July 14, 1954	113° F - July 14, 1954
2	112° F - July 18, 1954	113° F - July 12, 1954	108° F - July 12, 1954
3	111° F - July 24, 1934	111° F - July 15, 1936	108° F - July 13, 1954
4	110° F - July 12, 1954	111° F - July 25, 1934	108° F - July 18, 1954
5	110° F - August 9, 1934	111° F - July 18, 1954	108° F - July 30, 1986
6	110° F - July 20, 1934	111° F - July 30, 1980	107° F - July 17, 1954
7	108° F - July 28, 1930	110° F - July 1, 1980	106° F - July 23, 1901
8	108° F - August 8, 1934	110° F - August 29, 1984	106° F - July 24, 1934
9	108° F - July 23, 1934	110° F - August 9, 1934	106° F - July 15, 1936
10	108° F - July 14, 1936	110° F - August 10, 1934	106° F - July 18, 1936

Top 10 Coldest Days

	St. Louis	Columbia	Springfield
1	-23° F - January 29, 1873*	-26° F - February 12, 1899	-29° F - February 12, 1899
2	-22° F - January 5, 1884	-25° F - February 13, 1905	-22° F - February 13, 1905
3	-22° F - January 1, 1864*	-23° F - December 20, 1901	-19 F - January 12, 1918
4	-20° F - December 24, 1872*	-21° F - February 11, 1899	-18 F - January 11, 1918
5	-19° F - January 18, 1930	-20° F - December 22, 1989	-17 F - January 24, 1894
6	-18° F - February 13, 1905	-20° F - January 7, 1920	-17 F - January 18, 1930
7	-18° F - January 20, 1985	-20° F - February 9, 1899	-17 F - February 9, 1979
8	-17° F - January 12, 1918	-19° F - December 23, 1989	-16 F - February 11, 1899
9	-16° F - December 22, 1989	-19° F - December 25, 1983	-16 F - February 13, 1899
10	-16° F - February 12, 1899	-19° F - January 10, 1982	-16 F - December 23, 1899

* unofficial record

PROVISO: Readers should note that the section on heat waves and cold spells provides some examples of these extreme weather events over the years, but it does not purport to cover all the top hottest and top coldest days in the state. As illustrated in the charts above, the hottest days in the Missouri city of St. Louis, for example, have occurred predominantly in 1934 and 1954. The coldest low-temperature days recorded seem to have occurred predominantly in the late 1800s and the first two decades of the twentieth century.

Temperature records courtesy of the St. Louis Weather Service Forecast office.

Bibliography

I. Tornadoes

Primary Sources:

Television meteorologists contributed to all the sections of this book as primary sources by responding to a weather survey and also, in many cases, through e-mail and phone interviews: Kristen Cornett, Kent Ehrhardt, John Fuller, Dave Murray, and Cindy Preszler of St. Louis; Bryan Busby, Gary Lezak, Jeff Penner, and Lisa Teachman of Kansas City; Eric Aldrich, Josh deBerge, and Zach Paul of the Columbia–Jefferson City area; Gary Bandy and Dave Snider of the Joplin–Springfield area; and Brian Alworth and Bob Reeves of Cape Girardeau.

Also instrumental with interviews and primary source material: Pat Guinan, climatologist with the University of Missouri Extension Service, and James Kramper of the NOAA National Weather Service Office, who provided direction to weather photo archives and data sources in the public domain.

Secondary Sources:

Arnold, Jeff, "Starting Over: Pierce City Like a Ghost Town." *Springfield News-Leader*, July 6, 2003.

Bagnall, Norma. *On Shaky Ground: New Madrid Earthquake of 1811–1812*. Columbia: University of Missouri Press, 1996.

Ball, Jacqueline. *Tornado! The 1974 Super Outbreak*. New York: Bearport Publishing, 2005.

Brewer, Carolyn. *Caught in the Path: A Tornado's Fury, A Community's Rebirth*. Kansas City: Prairie Fugue Books, 1997.

Crone, Thomas. *Gaslight Square: An Oral History*. St. Louis: The William and Joseph Press, 2003.

Curzon, Julia, ed. *The Great Cyclone at St. Louis and East St. Louis, May 27, 1896*. Carbondale: SIU Press Reprint 1997.

Feknor, Peter. *The Tri-State Tornado*. Nebraska: iUniverse Inc., 2004.

Freier, George. *The Wonder of Weather*. New York: Random House, 1989.

Grazulis, Thomas. *Significant Tornadoes: 1680–1991*. Vermont: Environmental Films, 1993.

Hopewell, Menra. *Legends of the Missouri and Mississippi*. London: Ward Locke & Taylor, 1874.

Johnson, Wes. "1 Dead After Tornado Hits Southwest Missouri." *Springfield News-Leader* Homepage, January 7, 2008.

Johnson, Wes. "Tornado's Passenger in Media Cyclone." *Springfield News-Leader* Homepage, March 21, 2006.

Kelly Kasparie. "Tornado Season Begins Again." *Truman State University TruLife*, March 24, 2005.

Kirksville Weekly Graphic, "Kirksville Cyclone Account," May 12, 1899.

KMBC-TV Kansas City Homepage, "Violent Storms Kill 3 in Northern Missouri," May 13, 2009.

Little, Joan. "Tornado Kills Two and Injures 62 in Springfield, Mo." *St. Louis Post-Dispatch*, December 1, 1991.

Marshfield Mail, "Special Tornado Edition," May 1, 1930. Reprinted in the *Webster County Historical Society Journal*, April 1976.

Maryville Daily Forum, "Cape Girardeau Hit By Tornado," May 23, 1949.

MLH Graphics. *The Roaring Force . . . A Fourth To Remember*. Moberly, Mo.: MLH

Graphics & MCM/Proven Concepts, 1995.

Musick, John R. "In the Whirl of the Tornado." *Century Magazine*, August 1899.

Pearson, Allen, and Frederick Ostby. "The Tornado Season of 1974." *Weatherwise*, 1975.

Pickett, Calder. *Voices of the Past: Key Documents in American Journalism*. New York: John Wiley & Sons, 1977.

Poplar Bluff Daily Republican, "We Will Rebuild," May 11, 1927.

Rayo, Nina, Eric Eckert, and Jennifer Fillmer. "A Deadly Day." *Springfield News-Leader*, May 5, 2003.

Roxana Hegeman. "Tornadoes Kill At Least 22 in Three States." *St. Louis Post-Dispatch/ AP*, May 12, 2008.

St. Charles Cosmos Monitor, "Special Tornado Edition," February 1876.

Southeast Public Radio, KRCU of Southeast Missouri State University, "The 1949 Twister," 2003 Podcast.

Weems, Edward. *The Tornado*. Garden City, N.Y.: Doubleday, 1977.

II. Lightning And Hail

Primary Sources:

Primary sources for the lightning and hail section include interviews with reporter Bob Priddy of the capital press corps in Jefferson City, Ken Pettlton of Preferred Lightning Protection of Missouri, J. Seamus Donohue of Donohue's Lightning Protection of Missouri, David Robbins of Robbins' Lightning Protection of Missouri, Bud VanSickle of the U.S. Lightning Protection Institute, and Al Sedlacek, manager of Frontenac Hilton Hotel.

Additional interview sources include: Chief Gary Wirth of the Willard Fire Protection District, Chief Jim Eden of the Lee's Summit Fire Battalion, Rev. Kevin Hughes of the First Evangelical Church of Manchester, Rev. Matthew Bonk of the Rock Catholic Church of St. Louis, Chief Gary Warren of the Columbia Fire Department, Chief Gale Blomenkamp of the Boone County Fire Protection District, and Robert Lowery, mayor of the city of Florissant, as well as television meteorologists previously cited.

Secondary Sources:

Amantee, Michael. "Large Hail Criteria Look to Reduce Severe Thunderstorm Warnings." *Columbia Missourian*, March 10, 2009.

Bluestein, Howard. *Tornado Alley: Monster Storms of the Great Plains*. New York: Oxford University Press, 1999.

Corrigan, Don. *Show Me . . . Natural Wonders*. St. Louis: Reedy Press, 2007.

Cox, John D. *Weather for Dummies*. New York: Thunder's Mouth Press, 2006.

Crary, David. "Fatal Bolt Illuminates Boy Scouts' Questionable Record." *Los Angeles Times*, January 8, 2006.

Insurance Journal, "Damage Claims Reach 38,000 After Missouri Hailstorm," April 20, 2001.

Insurance Journal, "St. Louis Hailstorm Still Impacting Insurers," September 26, 2001.

Kansas City Star, "Lightning Strikes Missouri Fire Chief," July 16, 2004.

KMOV-TV St. Louis Homepage, "Two Missouri Pastors Survive Lightning Strike Without Injury," May 11, 2007.

Knight, Meredith. "Fact or Fiction: If the Sky Is Green, Run For Cover . . ." *Scientific American*, June 14, 2007.

Koenig, Marcia. "Pine Lawn Woman Drowns During Thunderstorm." *St. Louis Post-Dispatch*, October 9, 1984.

Joplin Globe, "Minor Flooding, Hail Reported in Area," May 1, 2009.

Powers, Ron. *Mark Twain: A Life*. New York: Simon & Schuster, 2005.

Scheff, Duncan. *Ice Storms and Hail Storms*. New York: Steadwell Books, 2002.

Simon, Seymour. *Lightning*. New York: Morrow Books, 1997.

USA Today, "Lightning Kills 3 People at a Funeral in Missouri," August 24, 2002.

III. Floods

Primary Sources:

Primary sources for the flood section include interviews with Kathy Hartman, vice president of Tiehen Group, Inc., Kansas City; Lillie Plowman, retired dispatcher, Shannon County Sheriff's Department, Eminence; Robin Brewer, operator of Circle B Cottage Cabins, Eminence; Jo Schaper, writer for the monthly *River Hills Traveler*; Julie Scerine, information officer, Missouri Highway Patrol; Colleen Reany, Webster University journalism student; and television meteorologists previously cited.

Secondary Sources:

Andreas, A.T. *History of the State of Kansas*. Atchison, Kan.: Atchison County Historical Society, 1976.

Auckley, Jim. "The 1995 Flood." *Conservationist*, August 1995.

Bagnall, Norma Hayes. *On Shaky Ground: The New Madrid Earthquakes of 1811–1812*. Columbia: University of Missouri Press, 1996.

Barry, John M. *Rising Tide: The Great Mississippi Flood of 1927 and How It Changed America*. Austin: Touchstone Publishing, 1998.

Brush Creek Bulletin, "Long Struggle To Tame Brush Creek," May/June 2004.

Corrigan, Don. "Storm Cleanup Continues. Residents Call It, 'Tornado of '82.'" *Webster-Kirkwood Times*, December 14, 1982.

Current Wave, "2 Canoeists Die On Jacks Fork," February 10, 1982.

Dallas Morning News, "Joplin Damaged By Flood," April 24, 1908.

Ekberg, Karl. *Colonial Ste. Genevieve*. Gerald, Mo.: Patrice Press, 1996.

Franzwa, Gregory. *The Story of Old Ste. Genevieve*. Gerald, Mo.: Patrice Press, 1990.

Hendryx, William. "Dam Break." *Reader's Digest*, July 2006.

Jefferson City Post-Tribune, "80,000 Are Homeless, Millions in Damages Along River Fronts," January 23, 1937.

McCoy, Kansas Joe, and Memphis Minnie. "When the Levee Breaks." Columbia Records, 1929.

Marsh, Don. *Flash Frames*. St. Louis: Reedy Press, 2008

Murphy, Kevin. "Flash Flood: Cleanup Continues After Sunday's Destructive Deluge." *Webster-Kirkwood Times*, September 19, 2008.

New York Times, "Gulf Storm Brings Flood To St. Louis," August 21, 1915.

NOAA News, "Kansas River Flood Set Records in 1951," July 12, 2001.

Penick, Jr., James. *The New Madrid Earthquakes*. Columbia: University of Missouri Press, 1981.

Pitluk, Adam. *Damned To Eternity*. Philadelphia: Da Capo Press, 2007.

Tomich, Jeffrey, and Paul Hampel. "A Sigh of Relief: Valley Park Levee Holds." *St. Louis Post-Dispatch*, March 28, 2008.

Washington Times/AP, "Muskrat Destroys Missouri Levee," June 28, 2008.

Zegel, Maureen. "Kirkwood Water Tested in Search for Dioxin." *Webster-Kirkwood Times*, January 11, 1983.

IV. Blizzards and Ice Storms

Primary Sources:

Primary sources for the blizzards and ice storms section include interviews with Kirk Hansen, public relations office of Fantastic Caverns, Springfield; Kelly Brown, restaurant manager, Lambert's Home of Throwed Rolls, Sikeston; and television meteorologists previously cited.

Secondary Sources:

Burt, Christopher. *Extreme Weather: A Guide and Record Book.* New York: W.W. Norton, 2004.
Daily Capital Jefferson City News, "Snow Brings Back Childhood To Adults," January 23, 1937.
Gibson McCarthy, Leslie. "Snap, Crackle, Pop." *South County Times,* December 8, 2006.
Holuska, Joshua. "Central U.S. Reeling From Ice Storms." *New York Times,* December 11, 2007.
Jefferson City Post-Tribune, "Cold and Snowstorm Worst in This Section," January 22, 1937.
O'Bryhim, Brendan, Amy Fischback, and Mike Harrington. "Kansas City's Icy Nightmare."
     Electric Wholesaling, March 1, 2002.
St. Louis Post-Dispatch, "The Blizzard of '82," Editorial, February 2, 1982.
Southeast Missourian, "New Yardstick, Blizzard of 1979," February 27, 1979.
University of Missouri Extension Service Homepage. "Persimmon Seeds Predict: Warm
     Weather, Above Average Snowfall in the Ozarks," November 7, 2008.

V. Heat Waves and Cold Spells

Primary Sources:

Primary sources for the heat waves and cold spells section include interviews with Pat Guinan, climatologist with the University of Missouri Extension Service; Dawn Mrad, veterinarian with Mid-Rivers Equine Center; James Kramper of the NOAA National Weather Service Office; Alan Dooley, public affairs officer for the St. Louis Region Army Corps of Engineers Office; Nelson "Spence" Spencer of the *Waterways Journal*; Steve Bircher, curator of mammals for the St. Louis Zoo; and television meteorologists previously cited.

Secondary Sources:

Bird, Christopher. *The Divining Hand: The 500-Year-Old Mystery of Dousing.* Altgen,
     Penn.: Whitford Press, 2000.
Burby, Liza N. *Heat Waves and Droughts.* New York: Rosen Publishing Group, 1999.
Cauchon, Dennis. "Accuracy of Windchill Factor Questioned." *USA Today,* February 17, 2000.
Karl, Thomas R., and Robert G. Quayle. "The 1980 Summer Heat Wave and Drought in
     Historical Perspective." *Weather Review,* 1981.
Luehrs, Sarah. "Hating The Heat? Be Glad It's 2007, Not 1936." *Columbia Missourian,*
     August 19, 2007.
McGuirk, J.P. "Planetary-Scale Forcing of the January 1977 Weather." *Science,* January 1978.
Merriman, Leah. "St. Louis May Be Boring, But That's Not a Bad Thing." *Webster
     University Journal,* August 30, 2007.
Namias, Jerome. "Anatomy of Great Plains Protracted Heat Waves." *Weather Review,* 1982.
Swanberg, W.A. *Pulitzer.* New York: Scribner, 1967.
St. Louis Post-Dispatch, "7 Horses Suffer Heat Exhaustion, 6 Revived By Rum," June 29, 1952.
St. Louis Post-Dispatch, "Storm Virtually Isolates City. No Relief Today," January 13, 1917.
St. Louis Post-Dispatch, "Turn It Off, Mr. Weatherman!" January 25, 1952.
Time, "The Big Freeze," January 31, 1977.

It should be noted that many of the NOAA, Library of Congress, and other archive photos used are meant strictly as illustrations of weather activity and do not always depict the actual weather events described in the text.

Section I: Tornadoes

Page 4: *photo courtesy of Library of Congress*
Page 6: *photo courtesy of Library of Congress*
Page 8: *photo courtesy of NOAA photo library*
Page 10: *photo courtesy of Don Roussin*
Page 12: *photo courtesy of NOAA photo library*
Page 14: *courtesy of Special Collections Photo Archives, Truman State University, Kirksville, Missouri*
Page 16: *map courtesy of NOAA photo library*
Page 18: *photo courtesy of NOAA weather reports*
Page 20: *photo courtesy of the Poplar Bluff Public Library*
Page 22: *photo courtesy of NOAA photo library*
Page 24: *photo courtesy of NOAA weather reports*
Page 28: *photo courtesy of NOAA weather reports*
Page 30: *satellite image courtesy of NOAA weather reports*
Page 32: *photo courtesy of NOAA photo library*
Page 34: *photo courtesy of NOAA photo library*
Page 36: *radar image courtesy of NOAA photo library*
Page 38: *radar image courtesy of NOAA weather reports*
Page 40: *photo courtesy of NOAA weather reports*
Page 42: *map courtesy of NOAA photo library*
Page 44: *radar image courtesy of NWS Doppler Radar and NOAA weather reports*
Page 46: *photo courtesy of NOAA photo library*

Section II: Lightning and Hail

Page 50: *photo courtesy of Library of Congress*
Page 52: *photo courtesy of Library of Congress*
Page 54: *photo courtesy of Missouri Department of Conservation*
Page 56: *photo courtesy of NOAA photo library*
Page 58: *photo courtesy of NOAA photo library*
Page 60: *photo courtesy of NOAA photo library*
Page 62: *photo courtesy of NOAA photo library*

Page 64: *photo courtesy of NOAA photo library*
Page 66: *photo courtesy of NOAA photo library*
Page 68: *radar image courtesy of NOAA weather reports*
Page 70: *photo courtesy of NOAA photo library*
Page 72: *photo courtesy of NOAA photo library*
Page 74: *photo courtesy of NOAA photo library*
Page 76: *photo courtesy of NOAA photo library*
Page 78: *photo courtesy of NOAA photo library*
Page 80: *photo courtesy of Tim Gunter*
Page 82: *radar image courtesy of NOAA photo library*

Section III: Floods

Page 86: *photo courtesy of NOAA photo library*
Page 88: *photo courtesy of FEMA*
Page 90: *photo courtesy of U.S. Geological Survey*
Page 92: *photo courtesy of Library of Congress*
Page 94: *photo courtesy of Diana Linsley of the Webster-Kirkwood Times*
Page 96: *photo courtesy of NOAA photo library*
Page 98: *photo courtesy of NOAA photo library*
Page 100: *photo courtesy of Library of Congress*
Page 102: *photo courtesy of Library of Congress*
Page 104: *photo courtesy of U.S Army Corps of Engineers*
Page 106: *photo courtesy of Missouri Department of Conservation*
Page 108: *Photo courtesy of Environmental Protection Agency (EPA)*
Page 110: *photo courtesy of Diana Linsley of the Webster-Kirkwood Times*
Page 112: *photo courtesy of Diana Linsley of the Webster-Kirkwood Times*
Page 114: *photo courtesy of NOAA weather reports*
Page 116: *photo courtesy of NOAA weather reports*
Page 118: *photo courtesy of Missouri Department of Conservation*
Page 120: *photo courtesy of Diana Linsley of the Webster-Kirkwood Times*
Page 122: *photo courtesy of FEMA*
Page 124: *photo courtesy of Diana Linsley of the Webster-Kirkwood Times*

Section IV: Blizzards and Ice Storms

Page 128: *photo courtesy of NOAA photo library*
Page 130: *photo courtesy of shutterstock*
Page 132: *photo courtesy of NOAA weather report*
Page 134: *photo courtesy of Diana Linsley of the*
Webster-Kirkwood Times
Page 136: *photo courtesy of shutterstock*
Page 138: *photo courtesy of shutterstock*
Page 140: *photo courtesy of shutterstock*
Page 142: *photo courtesy of Diana Linsley of the*
Webster-Kirkwood Times
Page 144: *photo courtesy of Diana Linsley of the*
Webster-Kirkwood Times
Page 146: *photo courtesy of FEMA/Michael Raphael*
Page 148: *photo courtesy of Diana Linsley of the*
Webster-Kirkwood Times

Section V: Heat Waves and Cold Spells

Page 152: *photo courtesy of Library of Congress*
Page 154: *photo courtesy of Library of Congress*
Page 156: *photo courtesy of shutterstock*
Page 158: *chart courtesy of NOAA*
Page 160: *photo courtesy of Diana Linsley of the*
Webster-Kirkwood Times
Page 162: *photo courtesy of Diana Linsley of the*
Webster-Kirkwood Times
Page 164: *photo courtesy of NOAA photo library*
Page 166: *photo courtesy of NOAA*
Page 168: *photo courtesy of NOAA photo library*
Page 170: *photo courtesy of Diana Linsley of the*
Webster-Kirkwood Times
Page 172: *photo courtesy of Robin Winkelman/Saint Louis Zoo*